IN THEIR OWN WORDS

LETTERS FROM A WORLD WAR II GI

IN THEIR OWN WORDS

LETTERS FROM A WORLD WAR II GI

BY JUDITH E. GREENBERG AND HELEN CAREY MCKEEVER

FRANKLIN WATTS
New York / Chicago / London / Toronto / Sydney

2550?

The authors wish to thank the families of Keith Winston, Edgar Schlossberg, Alma Klein Walensky, Jack McKeever, and John Albert Armistead for providing personal photographs.

Photographs copyright ©: VFW Magazine: pp. 17, 29, 75, 114, 128 top; Archive Photos/ Lambert: p. 19; The Bettmann Archive: pp. 24, 108, 112; UPI/Bettmann: pp. 43, 88, 95, 98, 106, 123, 133; Grolier Multimedia: p. 56; The American Red Cross: pp. 63, 81, 91, 117; U.S. Army Photo: p. 72, 103; Alan Gilberti, United States Holocaust Memorial Museum: p. 135.

Library of Congress Cataloging-in-Publication Data
  Winston, Keith, 1912–1970.
    Letters from a World War II GI / [edited] by Judith E. Greenberg and Helen Carey McKeever.
        p. cm. — (In their own words)
        Includes bibliographical references and index.
        ISBN 0-531-11212-8
        1. Winston, Keith, 1912–1970—Correspondence.
    2. Winston, Sarah—Correspondence. 3. World War,
    1939–1945—Personal narratives, American. 4. United
    States. Army. Infantry Regiment, 398th. Battalion, 2d—
    Biography. 5. United States. Army—Medical personnel—
    Biography. 6. World War, 1939–1945—Regimental
    histories—United States. 7. V-Mail. I. Greenberg, Judith E.
    II. McKeever, Helen Carey. III. Title. IV. Title: Letters from a
    World War Two GI V. Title: Letters from a World War 2 GI.
    VI. Series.
    D811.W4957 1995
    940.54'8173—dc20   94-46656
                                                                  CIP

ACKNOWLEDGMENTS

We are grateful to Sarah Winston, widow of Pfc. Keith Winston, United States Army, for generously permitting us to use her husband's letters and photographs in this book.

We also thank Archivist Sandy Cohen of the Jewish War Veterans' Museum in Washington, D.C., for his help and advice.

To the men and women who served our country in World War II and especially one soldier, Cpl. John R. McKeever, U. S. Army.

—HCM

In memory of Dr. Harold Greenberg, who during World War II was a captain in the U.S. Army and a recipient of a Bronze Medal.

—JEG

CONTENTS

IN THEIR OWN WORDS

LETTERS FROM A WORLD WAR II GI

MEETING KEITH WINSTON

On Memorial Day, 1993, President Clinton honored America's veterans of World War II by signing a proclamation making June 1 through June 7 the Week of National Observance for the Commemoration of the Fiftieth Anniversary of World War II. It was this war that defined the twentieth century and reshaped the world. With victory, the United States became the leader of the free world, worldwide colonialism ended, the nuclear age began, and science and technology made rapid advances.

In a White House ceremony, President Clinton said,

As we observe the fiftieth anniversary of World War II, our country must remember and honor the millions who defended democracy and defeated aggression. The freedoms we enjoy today are results of our victory over aggression, and the effort the United States makes today to work with all other nations who love and believe in freedom

11

*are a testimony to the wisdom of the lessons
learned then. . . . The nation owes a special debt
to the millions of men and women who took up
posts at home or abroad to secure our defenses or
to fight for our freedom.*

The president might very well have been talking about the soldier who wrote the letters in this book. Using Keith Winston's letters to his wife as a starting point, you will gain a better understanding of the history and lessons of World War II. You will appreciate how the United States armed forces fighting around the world were joined by Americans at home, who also worked for the common cause of preserving freedom.

Although approximately 16 million men and women served in the United States armed services during World War II, there are fewer complete collections of letters and firsthand accounts of life in the military than you might expect. One reason for this lack of primary source material is that the government did not allow soldiers and sailors to include any information in their letters that might end up helping the German and Japanese enemies. To make certain this didn't happen, military censors read the letters sent home from overseas, and blacked out or cut out sensitive information.

Keith Winston's wife kept all of her husband's letters in the order they were received and, even though they were censored, his observations were so acute that they give us a fairly complete portrait of an American soldier in wartime.

Many men and women in the armed forces wrote letters to family and friends about what they saw and felt. But Keith Winston's letters form an extraordinary human document. He wrote of his fears and his intense longing for home, and yet his words also convey his commitment to freedom, and the need to defeat America's enemies.

Keith Winston was inducted into the army in March

Keith Winston, recruit, U.S. Army, 1944

1944. At age thirty-two, he was older than the average GI. His letters written home to his wife Sarah and his two young sons record his day-to-day observations of army life and his experiences as a combat medic in Europe.

Keith Winston was born in Philadelphia, Pennsylvania, on October 28, 1912. He was very young when his father died, and because his family was poor, he was sent to a charitable boarding school for fatherless boys for his early education. When he reached college age, he was financially unable to complete college and helped his mother start a business instead. He became an insurance underwriter and married Sarah in 1932. Together they had two sons, Neil and David.

Winston joined the 100th Infantry Division after completing basic training and then served as a combat medic in the 398th Infantry Regiment, a part of the U.S. Seventh Army that was involved in the invasion of France and Germany.

Winston received the Purple Heart for wounds suffered in combat and also the Bronze Star for meritorious achievement in action.

After the war was over, Keith Winston once again took up his career in insurance. He also did some freelance work as a photojournalist, and collaborated with his wife in editing and writing magazine articles. He died on March 20, 1970, at the age of fifty-seven.

As you begin to read Keith Winston's letters, we hope you realize that they contain moments of unguarded intimacy because he was writing not for publication, but for his wife and family. Remember, too, that he is putting on paper the conversations he most likely would have had with his wife if she had been there beside him. We have chosen not to alter his abbreviations and symbols unless clarity demanded it. On occasion, we provided additional information to help readers understand some of the events and elements of wartime fifty years ago.

ARMY
BASIC TRAINING
MARCH TO AUGUST 1944

25 March 1944

Here I am in New Cumberland, Pa. and so far they're taking good care of me. Very low when I left but it helped to run into two boys examined with me—and just what I needed. One was married eleven years, has two kids. With few exceptions all the men are fathers. Glad you stayed home with the children. It was pretty hard leaving, and it would have been harder on both if you drove down with me.

Am now resting in my bunk in a dormitory of 48 bunk-type beds, waiting for supper bell. Everyone seems especially friendly, both inductees and officers (like we're in the same boat together, boys) and that makes things easier. After dinner I'm heading for the Post Theater to see movie. Lights go out at 9:15 but we're permitted around post till 11. We get up at 6 A.M. However, remember all these are this Reception Camp's rules, and in five or six days we're due to be shipped to a permanent camp. If I'm lucky enough to be here till next Saturday I believe I can get a pass home for a day or two. But make no plans.

So much for me. From my experience today, being so blue and low, then mingling and feeling better, I'm suggesting that you get out of the house early, see people and do things—even if the house suffers. I know it will help considerably.

Just came from supper—hot dogs, salad, soup, peaches, coffee. Everything is clean and spotless—not like you'd expect in an Army camp. So far it feels like some sort of vacation and I kind of feel guilty because you're having the full responsibility. Dear, don't hold back on any problems, for in that way we can share some responsibilities together even though we're apart. It will help us both. Keep your chin up, kid. With all my love.

TYPICAL ARMY-ISSUED EQUIPMENT

1 dufflebag, two pair underwear, 2 canteen cups, one khaki-colored shirt, four cotton handkerchiefs, two green terry cloth towels, 2 pair green cotton socks, knife, fork, spoon, footlocker, Eisenhower jacket, 1 broad webbing belt, 1 sleeveless undershirt, 1 green wool blanket, 1 mess kit, one canteen, 1 pair rolled cotton socks, 1 dress belt, first aid kit, white haversack, 2 helmets, 1 pair green wool gloves, 1 green wool neck scarf, 1 brown wool shirt, 1 pair matching slacks, 1 brown dress tie, 1 brown Garrison cap, 1 entrenching tool, 20 cans of C rations, Dog Tags, 1 toothbrush, 1 Colgate toothpaste, 4 packets each coffee, cream, salt, sugar, 1 sewing kit, 1 Army New Testament, 1 can opener, 1 Basic Field Manual, Soldier's Handbook, 1 tent with 3 wooden tent pegs

29 March

Just received your first letter and I, too, can say it was a morale builder. Enjoyed every word, including

With uniforms and equipment issued,
recruits began basic training.

Neil's and for the first time in my life, read a letter over
and over again. I hope you mean it when you say you're
doing well. Please don't hesitate to tell me anything, or
about any problems that come up.

Since you're interested in all the details—here's

what's happening. Yesterday we received uniforms—complete outfits summer and winter clothing of every sort, money bag and things too numerous to mention. In the afternoon we were shown Army movies from 1–4 P.M., revealing the hard, bare facts of syphilis in action and it was sickening. And various other Army pictures exclusively made for instruction purposes. After supper went to the Post Theater and enjoyed a double feature.

Today I received needles for typhoid and tetanus. While the injection was hardly felt, the aftereffects are annoying but not painful.

Tomorrow our unit is on KP [Kitchen Police] all day—14 hours. That means serving food, helping prepare it, washing dishes, etc. Most of the boys don't mind, and before we leave, everyone gets a turn at it.

I'm expecting to be shipped out any day now and will not know when I leave, even to the extent of an hour's notice. If it happens before I get a pass, I'll try (don't depend on it) to phone you. I won't know where—just that I'm going.

Keep chin up, Darling. If any emergency develops call this camp 7 P.M. person to person. Explain to operator it's an emergency, but don't call unless it is, as it requires an OK by proper authorities—they might even call up FDR [President Franklin Delano Roosevelt] first! Who knows! Remember now to get out and see a show once in awhile. Does the car need gas? Watch it closely on small speedometer. The B coupon is good for 5 gallons. Neil, I'm looking forward to some of those school papers you promised to send, and thank you for wanting to send the dollar Aunt Bess gave you, and if Daddy ever needs it he'll write you. How's that? My love to you all.

In January 1942, rationing was established to provide a fair system of distributing scarce goods. Every family was issued ration books with stamps or

*At home, ration books became
part of everyday shopping.*

coupons to use along with money to pay for rationed
items. Not only gasoline was rationed. By the end of
the war, twenty grocery-store items were rationed,
including sugar, coffee, meat, butter, and cheese.
Paper products and shoes were also rationed. Nylon

stockings were nearly impossible to get and women learned to put makeup on their legs and draw lines up the backs, to imitate the stockings with seams of the day! Some goods were in short supply because they were needed for the troops. Others came from countries that were under seige by our enemies or were under control of the enemy. Everyone was encouraged to "use it up; wear it out; and make do"; an attitude that is not very different from our recycling ideas of today.

1–2 April, En route

Here it is 10 P.M. Saturday night, and if my writing looks shaky and hard to decipher it's because I'm lying on an upper berth heading South toward Georgia or Florida (probably Ft. Benning) but these troop trains travel under strict secrecy and no one knows anything except the Capt. and Lt. We left 4 P.M. and 500 men are aboard. There's no question but what I'm headed for an Infantry camp, but don't let that discourage you since almost everyone gets Infantry basic and then transferred to specialized schools, etc. after the end of the training period.

Wasn't allowed to call home as I'd hoped, and I guess you had half a hope that I'd be seeing you over the weekend. Well, Friday I applied for a pass with all the other eligibles, and everything was all set. Then Saturday morning we received our call. You can imagine how brokenhearted I was—since we may as well face it—we won't see each other again till the end of basic, a minimum of 13 weeks. Remember, Dear, thousands are in the same boots. Try to be a good soldier and take it. All my love.

4 April, Camp Blanding, Fla.

Well, Dearest, today we're feeling a little better and beginning to get the swing of things. Here I am at Camp

Blanding, a far cry from New Cumberland where you were treated as an individual and not a number. This is Army. No question about that. And I must admit the abrupt change is pretty unsettling, plus the disappointment of not being closer to home. I find it hard to take the harsh, rigid discipline handed out. I know I'm here to stay so I try to make the best of it, rationalizing that there's a good reason for every bonehead order that comes through from some featherbrained young Lt. [lieutenant] just beginning to feel the magic of his authority. And it does make things a little easier.

Our Sgt. [sergeant] is stern and grim but with it all he has a quality and ability that commands respect, and it's men like him who really make the Army.

This week and next is geared chiefly to drilling and you can't imagine how tough it is. Yet there's some satisfaction at the end of the day when you've executed the commands properly, and usually feel good physically. Also we have an hour of calisthenics daily, such as you see in the movies. If you're not exhausted after all this, you're superhuman. Incidentally, I was appointed squad leader (15 men).

About how I live—we have a hut, similar to a lake cabin and five men share it. My bunkmates are fine fellows—all married with children, and contrary to 95% of Army men, rarely cuss. The hut (so-called) is screened in all around and protected by flaps. The Army requires they be open on two sides at all times, but generally they're open all around as the days down here are pretty warm. Already after two days, with half the day cloudy and rainy, I'm beginning to tan and will probably be dark when you see me. We wear suntans—our official summer uniform.

There's a possibility I'll be transferred to the Clerk's School. The men who interviewed me said they'd recommend the change and gave me a #1 rating. I'd still get

6 weeks of Infantry which includes drilling and rifle instruction.

So much for me—now to my main concern. You and the boys. Are you getting down to a system yet? Remember the importance of getting out of the house. I miss you all so much. Dear, lights are about to go out so I'll close with all my love to you all.

5 April, Co. "A"—229th I. T. B., Camp Blanding, Fla.

Note the new address—which means I'm now a member of the Clerk School. I believe it may be easier than Infantry training since we receive only 6 weeks of basic instead of 17. After that we get 9 weeks of school which includes practice in Army offices throughout the camp. Then 2 weeks of maneuvers to finish—and then an assignment in this camp or elsewhere. Your letters will reach me now, Dear, and I'll be looking forward to them.

8 April

I've been wanting to write you a number of times about how I really feel. I wanted to write—and then I didn't want to write. But you'd be the only one who could understand what mental anguish I'm going through. I know you'd understand how it feels to have a paining and aching and gnawing heart inside a completely exhausted body. A condition which exists frequently. But that's all I'll say along these lines—and already I'm sorry I said it. Now I'll tell you what's going on.

In the first place, I got into the Infantry. I and a few hundred thousand more were immediately going to get a transfer out of this branch. But that was pure fantasy. The very first thing they told us was "You cannot transfer out of the Infantry, so don't try it—there are no exceptions." And we learned soon enough these were the hard facts. Well, after reclassification I was transferred to the Infantry Clerk School and now I consider myself fortunate in getting here since the platoon is made up of 75% family men—mostly all businessmen or professionals, and I can truthfully say, as a unit, they're about the smartest bunch I have ever run into.

11 April

Receiving mail is a big problem here, and a disappointment. It's all mixed-up. I'm not getting any, and one of my bunkmates hadn't received a letter since leaving home for the induction center—then this morning he got 13 at once!

Well, Honey, today the real training started and I want to tell you it's rugged. In one day I've exercised more than in any one month of my life. We're up at 5:45—breakfast at 6:15, and by 7:30 we've eaten, and barracks are in first-class condition. Then every hour is taken up with some sort of drill, exercises, rifle-practice, rifle cleaning. This is to be our routine throughout six long weeks; we're told there will be back-crawling, hiking with packs on our backs, crawling on ground with live machine-gun bullets whizzing over our heads.

Today my teeth were examined and I'll be having them fixed for the next few weeks.

Thank God for the movies! Tonight I went—cost $.15, 10 tickets for $1.20. There are ten movie houses to choose from if you want to walk.

So far the evenings have been delightful—hope it continues. Many flowers are in bloom—petunias and lilacs in particular and many more. This Florida sun would certainly be good for you—and your presence would do a lot more good than the sun—but of course I'm only dreaming. How are my boys? I look forward to Neil's letters. And David? I guess he wouldn't know me now. God bless you all.

Drills filled the recruits' training days.

Going to the movies for relaxation is mentioned several times in the letters from Keith Winston. This pastime was a favorite among the men and women serving in the armed forces and those at home. The movies allowed the viewer a short period of "escape" from wartime worries. The themes of the movies were often patriotic or fanciful. Even the hit music of the

1940s often had a patriotic or even a military theme. Some of the favorites included: "Stars and Stripes Forever," "Boogie Woogie Bugle Boy," "Comin' in on a Wing and a Prayer," This Is the Army Mr. Jones," "When the Lights Go on Again," "You'd Be So Nice to Come Home To," "I'll Be Home for Christmas," "It's the V that Stands for Victory," "Marching through Berlin," "Praise the Lord and Pass the Ammunition," and "Rosie the Riveter."

17 April

Today 5 letters, including Neil's, and since I hadn't heard from you yesterday, I don't have to tell you what it does for me. Neil, I showed your paper to all my soldier friends and they thought I had a pretty smart son. Keep them coming. How do you like the study of China? Did you know that China is one of our Allies? They're fighting Japan with us. Daddy's keeping busy down here and misses you very much, but I hope I can come home in 3 or 4 months, and if this terrible war ends, maybe sooner.

Honey, as to where my battalion is sent—including overseas—there's still a glimmer of hope I won't have to go. I base this on the questioning of pre-Pearl Harbor fathers by the Sgt. And today the Lt. said that fathers would be the last to leave the country. However, things change rapidly in the Army and just don't hope too much for anything.

Down here the meals are on the porky side. I'd say in about 80% of our meals pork is used. Sunday dinner is about our best meal—chicken or turkey and ice cream.

Today we were learning how to use the bayonet and hand grenade. God! Can you picture me putting a bayonet through another man? But they tell us—over and over again—if we don't, they'll do it to us. (Goodnight and pleasant dreams!)

22 April

Couldn't write yesterday, Friday, as we have rifle inspection Saturday A.M. and it requires many hours to get the rifles in shape. Our Lt. has the reputation of being the toughest in our Bn. [battalion] on inspection and if you don't pass you lose "pass rights" for the weekend, besides being hit with an extra detail. You can't begin to imagine the importance they attach to this, and I must admit we were all worried we wouldn't pass.

You see, the rifle is rather intricate and has to be just so—not one grain of sand can be found (down here there's only sand—no dirt), no rusty parts, just the proper thickness of oil on certain parts, etc.

After he inspected mine he said, "You have a good rifle." That, from him, was like a commendation from a 5-star General since he rarely says a good word, and you can bet I'm a happy soldier today.

Well, 2 weeks of training are over—one-third—and we're not unhappy about it. It seems to go quickly in spite of the pace. Will put this letter in the mail now, Sweetheart, and hope to write again tomorrow, Sunday, when we sleep about an hour longer.

1 May

As you know, we're learning to shoot the rifle. You have to give them credit for their expertise in teaching us how to fire, and if this preliminary instruction means anything, they tell me I'll be an "expert," an appraisal which somehow failed to rouse my sporting blood under these conditions. Anyway, to give you an idea how it works—there's a movable bull's-eye 200 yards out. The soldier looks through the rifle, which is placed in a permanent position, and by signaling another soldier 200 yards away, the bull's-eye is moved up, down, over, etc. until the rifle is aiming perfectly at the target. Then he signals the soldier that he has focused, and a mark is made in the center of the bull's-eye. The bull's-eye is moved twice more and the same procedure is repeated; if the three marks almost coincide, the novice rifleman is considered a candidate for an "expert." While I was told mine was one of the best, when we use real bullets next week it could change the picture. Rifle practice is like a sport until the thought hit me that this isn't shooting at carnival targets, but is aimed at shooting people and it leaves me cold.

Wednesday our Co. [company] is scheduled to march and drill at the retreat parade, which means we'll march with band music and be reviewed by the General. It's amusing how excited the officers are about it, like kids, ordering us to practice every spare moment.

Today our Sgt. told us he was promoted and will be leaving us. You might recall, from the beginning he commanded our respect, and we felt bad to see him go as we all thought the world of him—unlike that swinish Captain who only aroused our contempt.

Got paid today—$9.85. How they arrived at that enormous figure I'll never know, and there's not much you can do about it.

Just spoke to you, Sweetheart—how I enjoyed it. It felt so good to hear your voice—and there's one soldier who's feeling a little better tonight.

10 May
It's surprising how much money I spend down here— every night will find me at the PX [Post Exchange]. After a hot, weary march we all look for refreshment—ice-cream (a pint no less), drinks, cake, and always something extra like writing paper, soap (plenty, too), foot powder, shoe polish, brush, movies. However, I believe I'll make out when I receive my first full pay—about $13.00 net. Your enclosure of $5 sure came in handy. This past weekend in Jax [Jacksonville, Florida] convinced me to

stay right here unless I've a definite thing to do or place to go. It gives me a chance to rest and I'm ready for what Monday brings.

After supper I usually lie down for half an hour, go to PX to refresh a bit, then spend two exciting hours cleaning the rifle. Finish about 10 P.M., then a bath, clean mess kit, wash socks, shave, and try to hit the bed by 11, but it's usually closer to 12. Then up again at 4:45. That's just this week, but so far with half gone I don't feel any the worse for it. If I miss writing I know you'll understand.

16 May

Am now awaiting a truck ride to a firing range. The purpose: to acquaint us with firing at unknown distances requiring accurate estimation as to yardage. For the various ranges the rifle has to be adjusted accordingly. It's quite a learning experience.

Since I wrote the above I've been on the range and back again. We'd been working hard in the hot sun for 3 solid hours, and finally given a rest. When we started to drink from our canteens, the water was literally so hot very few boys could take it. However, set aside in a shady spot were three 5-gallon cans of cool water for the officers. The guys saw this and about a dozen went over and filled their canteens.

When the Captain discovered it he questioned the men but no one would admit to their "guilt." He turned blue with anger and ordered us all to walk back in the hot sun—a distance of 7 miles—even though we were slated for a truck ride back.

I showered immediately to revive myself and got dressed but was too tired to eat so went to the PX for a quart of milk and crackers.

Tomorrow again in the field all day and will be having our first taste of C rations. They come in cans, and the boys say they're very satisfying.

28

*Recruits were introduced to type-C field
rations during training maneuvers.*

C rations were canned field rations. They consisted of
precooked food packed in sealed cans. The food
could be eaten hot or cold. Each ration was intended
to provide a number of meals. It was made up of 3
cans of meat and vegetables, and 3 cans containing

crackers, sugar, and powdered coffee. The army also issued K rations that came in a waterproof box about the size of a Cracker Jack box. The K rations consisted of dried foods such as crackers, candy, preserved foods, and also included matches and cigarettes.

27 May

After chow today, our Company was called on to witness something that will be difficult to ever forget. Two companies of 360 men came off bivouac last week—which means 2 weeks of maneuvers. They eat and sleep there for the entire period.

It's a strict rule that empty ration cans are to be gathered and brought back to camp by truck for salvage. The purpose: to discourage wild pigs from inundating the area. There are hordes of them and they seem to be everywhere. Well, anyway, one of the boys dug one of his cans into the ground—probably eating between meals and tried to get rid of it some way.

That was the last day on bivouac. Early the next day, as soon as the group returned, the Company was informed that a hole four feet deep was dug by pigs immediately after they left. Well, the whole group, one by one, was questioned and since the "guilty" man would not own up, the entire 360 footsore, weary men and 10 officers were commanded to walk the 34 miles back as punishment.

Thirty-four miles because of one man's infraction of rules. Being forced to witness these desolate men starting off was a searing experience I'll long remember.

The boys here are a great bunch of guys, and the more I see of them the better I like them. You've never seen a group from so many walks of life that seem to have so much in common. For instance, businessmen, lawyers, clerks, laborers, farmers, men of position and money, men with little or nothing, but there's a genuine bond—you might call it survival—that brings every type of man together. With few exceptions, everyone is a gentleman.

6 June

Darling! Today is D-Day and I'm so happy I could bawl. The invasion will be a success—it has to be. None of us see it any other way.

At 5:45 this morning there was suddenly a lot of loud cheering outside but we paid little attention. Then someone from another hut ran in yelling, "The Invasion is on," and five guys, as one, jumped up to turn the radio on. It was true—and I wasn't the only guy who hid a tear. This is the day we all dreamed about. And now that it's here, we're all going about our duties—which continue, come what may—with lighter hearts and a renewed hope, for the Invasion will not fail.

The above was written early today. It's now 11 P.M. and I just returned from the movies. Saw The Eve of St. Mark. I urge you to see it as it gives you some idea of Army life—what the men do and think and feel.

Well, it's been quite a day all around. Goodnight, Sweetheart.

The expression D-Day was used in WW II to mark the date set for the Allied landing on German-held territory. D-Day was June 6, 1944, when the Allies invaded Normandy, France. On this day, 176,000 troops, along with thousands of tons of military equipment, poured ashore to start the campaign to liberate Western Europe from Nazi control.

12 June

Darling, did you hear Walter Winchell [popular radio newscaster and newspaper columnist of the 1940s] last night? He said Germany's position is much worse than it appears and he predicts they'll be out of the war within 6 weeks. I didn't hear him myself, but that's what the boys told me and I hope they got the facts straight.

Lately we've been chewing over the possibilities of where (what section) we might get placed—such as personnel section of a company, battalion, regiment headquarters, or even field cadre. The general feeling among the men is that they'd like to be shipped out of here and take their chances on a location closer to home. The way it works now, all men are shipped to Fort Meade or Fort Ord, and then reclassified. After this training, my classification should (and little doubt will) be Army Clerk-Skilled. Then you're shipped to camps where you're needed—if not out of the country. At the present writing, men over 32 years of age and those with families are not shipped out [of the country]. My pipe-dream is that the German part of this war comes to an abrupt end and the government starts discharging men fast—and that I get transferred to some point up north where they have huge administrative sections and need thousands of office help. Even if kept in the Army, which is far from unlikely, and at one of those points, it wouldn't be so bad, would it? Of course all this is just thinking out loud—and if you were in the Army you'd know what I mean. It seems they take the most logical idea, turn it around and do exactly the opposite. But we learn to adjust and try to find the "humor" in it.

19 June

Today a very long and wonderful letter—and its effect could be classified as a morale builder for a very low and lonesome soldier. Now this soldier's morale is not so low; he's still lonesome, but feels better.

Now 6 weeks and 4 days left to finish training, and believe me, we're all counting the days. Heard the 9-mile speed march will be eliminated and you know no one is shedding tears over that. It was tough enough doing 5.

I'm sure the decision was reached because of the intense heat. The first platoon made it last week (9 miles) and only half were able to finish. Others dropped along the way from exhaustion and heat prostration.

You know, Honey, it has always been a secret desire of mine to study medicine some day, and I feel I could make out well in it. This might surprise you but I'm writing for college catalogs now. I'm crazy—there go the bonds [savings bonds]!

Your letters are my mainstay. I haven't realized their significance until recently—for without question they do more to keep me going than anything else. Goodnight, my family.

28 June

It's early in the morning and a dozen boys of the first platoon, who graduated Saturday, left for home. You can't realize what we were feeling, watching them leave for the train, happy as kids, in direct contrast to the gloom of those watching. Well, our day is coming. After I go to the next camp I'd be eligible for a furlough but I'm still hoping things will be over by then. Eighteen-year-olds are sent to Alabama (Camp Rucker), but I think pre-Pearl Harbor fathers are sent to Fort Meade [Maryland], reclassified, then sent wherever they're needed. If I'm sent to Meade, wouldn't it be great if I were stationed there. Everything in the Army seems to be HOPE and LUCK. One of our group whose eyesight is not up to par, but otherwise as good as the best of us, was classified "Class C" and permanently assigned here. He's one of the lucky ones as he lives a couple of hundred miles from here, and his wife often visits.

3 July

Monday, and the start of another week. Have I ever told you how it feels getting up at 4 A.M. to go on some schedule detail? This morning was typical, and I think interesting. We went on the bayonet obstacle course two miles from our area. There's not a word among the men as they're getting ready. They're still sleepy and have their hands full getting into the proper regalia (light field pack, raincoats), filling canteens, etc. There's grim silence—as often pictured in the movies right before a group heads into battle—waiting for the zero hour. The total darkness helps to produce that effect.

Then, 5:30 we're on our way—marching through the dark. I can't quite describe how it feels—our minds are hazy and unclear, and you almost imagine you're in Italy or somewhere heading for the front. As light begins to appear we start snapping back to reality. Despite the raincoats we're drenched, but by this time it doesn't matter. We march along like zombies—and the strange, weird thing is that regardless of the obstacles we march right through them. This morning we pushed through puddles up to our ankles as if it were clean, dry land.

I received the ration points and will make good use of them over the weekend—also the package from Gimbels. [A well-known, large department store] It was just like a grab-bag—one box cookies, one of crackers, a glass jar of chicken, one of turkey, a can of sardines, jar of peanut candy, stuffed olives. Thanks very much, Sweetie.

12 July

Twenty-four more days and the course will be over. I count every day, and every day seems to be longer than the one before.

Did I ever tell you about Special Orders, and how they work? Let's say that Washington, D.C., decides they want 100 men—50 riflemen, 25 laborers, 15 cooks and 10 clerks sent to Fort Dix. They telegraph our camp which houses an elaborate filing system. They push a number, 610—that's the Army file # for riflemen—and also 50 which gives them the first 50 riflemen, and so on down to #40 (Clerk file #) and get the first 10 clerks available.

The names, rank, serial number, Company and file number of occupation are listed in this general order with instruction as to what camp they're being transferred to, and dates, etc. My special order will be somewhat different. The Washington telegram will probably read—send 200 trainees who have just completed basic to Fort Meade. And at Meade the above procedure would follow after I returned from the furlough.

Right now I'm at my practical work office where I'll be mimeographing General Orders, as 2700 men are to be shipped. Have a feeling that orders for our 2nd platoon will be included—they're in their 17th week, graduating in 3 days.

Later. As I thought, the special orders came down from the 2nd platoon and they're due to ship Tuesday, 3 days after graduation. I hope I'm that lucky.

When I see my name on such an order and am safely ensconced on the train, I'll feel like a new man. Until then, I'm just anticipating.

15 July

We're getting prepared for our bivouac trek. We carry a heavy pack consisting of a tent, accessories that go with it, blanket, raincoat, mess equipment, helmet, shoes, rations. It weighs 55 pounds besides a 10-lb. rifle. We start our 18-mile hike Monday 3 A.M.—breakfast at 2 A.M. Well, after this it will be practically over, and if that's the case—bring it on.

Thought I'd tell you something of the infiltration course while it's fresh in my memory. Yesterday we went through it twice. I wasn't the least bit concerned until a day or so before, when the Corporal (in trying to assure us everything was OK) kept telling us to be sure and keep our behinds down, and if we bumped into anybody who was hurt or petrified (literally) from fright, don't stop—and if a bullet "ricocheted" (hit something and bounced back) on us, it would only burn and couldn't hurt us, etc. Then I became somewhat nervous. Our new Lt., in an effort to raise our spirits, told us they used to shoot bullets 18 inches off the ground, but too many men were being killed, so they raised it to 19 inches. Kidding, of course. But now that it's over I can tell you that occasionally some soldier does get killed.

Well, we were finally led to the slaughterhouse and given the signal to "go over the top." To say I crawled is putting it mildly. I practically dug a hole and crawled along like a mole. It finally got to the point where I was so fagged out [exhausted] that I forgot all about the bullets whizzing overhead and just concentrated on pushing on to the end. It wasn't just plain "crawling." We had to maneuver through a tangle of barbed wire and climb over logs. I was soaked with sweat and covered with sand, which was everywhere, and the only way I could get out of there was to complete the course, for if you stand, it would be for the last time. So, exhausted or not, you've got to inch on. Well, I'm writing this letter so you know I finally made it, but it took a few hours to recoup from the ordeal. It was one of the toughest grinds we were ever put through.

To make the "run" more realistic they kept blowing off dynamite charges that just about deafened you and shook the ground like the rumblings of an earthquake. The main effect was to unnerve you, but I realized that keeping my wits was the essential thing, and, believe me, I worked at it mighty hard.

At night it was easier physically, but harder on the nerves, chiefly because in my lane (there were 10) was a row of dynamite charges and boy, when they went off, every few seconds, it was murderous.

In a grim sense it was thrilling, too, because they

use tracer bullets which leave a trail of smoke and fire, and at night, skimming overhead, it was a fascinating sight. I believe if it weren't for those hellish dynamite charges, I might have lain out there a bit just watching the bullets.

25 July

Last night I saw a spectacle that will be hard to forget—the working of an Infantry Battalion on defense. They shot tracer bullets (impressive and noisy), and demonstrated in action cannons, rifles, machine guns and mortars—separately, then simultaneously. After witnessing that display it's not hard to understand why our boys are doing so well. Again this morning we watched an Infantry Battalion on the offense—and boy! when you see those riflemen out there in the midst of fire, you begin to feel mighty good about being transferred to the Clerk School. A rifleman has a very important and dangerous job, and believe me, every infantryman in battle is a real hero.

Next day—26 July—I dug a foxhole 2 x $3^{1}/_{2}$ x 6 feet deep in the sweltering sun—and fast—with gas attacks all afternoon; and after all that, had to fill it up again.

Only 3 more days out here and you know I'm not sorry. Seem to be having a hell of a time sleeping on this ground. I have yet to get the first good night of rest.

2 August

Good news today. I'm on order to ship out of here next Tuesday, August 8 at 8:30 A.M., as of this writing. Jim J. [James N. Johnston, Keith Winston's roommate during basic training] at "classification" sneaked a preview. Tomorrow morning when I get it to mimeograph, I'll have all the facts.

Am to get 13 days, including travel time, but there

are a few more details I don't know of yet. My next letter will tell you, I hope.

I've been reading about the PRT [Philadelphia Rapid
Transit] strike in Philly, re: the first trial run of eight
Negroes being trained as motormen. I hope by now it's
settled. The world is full of prejudice, and it doesn't seem
that it will ever change. It's very sad, but I'm afraid, true.

I'm thinking about next week when I'll be home!
Maybe we could spend 2 or 3 evenings out, at some good
hotel, dining and dancing with some friends.

Don't mention anything to the family about my coming home, otherwise they'll be planning to entertain me,
which I absolutely won't accept. Again, until tomorrow,
my Love.

COMBAT
TRAINING
AUGUST TO OCTOBER 1944

On August 28, 1944, Keith Winston was moved from
Fort Meade to Fort Bragg, North Carolina, to join the
100th Infantry Division. The "Century Division" consisted mostly of troops from the northeastern part of
the United States, Virginia, and the Carolinas. In
1943, the division was engaged in advanced combat preparation and its ranks were repeatedly deplet-
ed when overage soldiers were transferred out, and
when division members were sent overseas to
replace soldiers wounded and killed in other military
units. Keith Winston was among the last group of
infantrymen sent to the Century Division to bring it
up to full strength before the entire division was sent
overseas.

1 September, Fort Bragg, N.C.

The war news still continues to look pretty good—
but it has to look even better, doesn't it, so we can always
be together again. This Camp is tremendous and unless

Keith Winston was assigned to the 100th
Infantry Division, at Fort Bragg, North Carolina.

you have a car, it's just about impossible to see it all.
The Division area I'm in houses between 7,500 and 10,000
men. We have one Service Club and 2 theaters—and that
seems inadequate, especially since the same picture
plays in both theaters the same night, necessitating leaving the area if you've already seen it.

There's no training here at camp. Schedules are
issued from day to day, e.g., today they raked through
the records and listed those who hadn't fired the car-
bine or M-1 rifle on the transition range (there are numerous types of ranges) during the last six months, and the
Army requires it every 6 months.

Other days we have lectures, and exercise almost
daily, but in the form of games—baseball, football, etc.
I just mention this to let you know I'm not overworking.
My only problem is being away from home. Think I'll
close now, Sweets. All my love.

5 September

I'm contented now, as your letter is before me. With it, my morale is lifted as high as it's possible under these conditions.

You ask if Jim is in my Division. Yes—although in a different regiment. There are three—397, 398, 399. Although closely aligned, they're divided for administration and training purposes.

Neil's observation of your "worried" look touched me so much. He's really a great little guy, with all the little problems he creates. Re: the Infantile Paralysis [polio] scare. By all means send him to school. I don't believe in overcautiousness, as that often turns out to be just as bad.

It burns me up the way the Army operates. All a GI has to look forward to is evenings and weekends. Why, then, do officers and non-coms [noncommissioned officers] just wait for those periods to pile on the extra details, especially with little or no training around. They hold those few free hours over your head and practically make you sweat for them—after they've shaved it down to a minimum.

Try not to worry, and always remember I'm thinking of you, and love you.

The term GI has an odd origin. It was originally used by military bookkeepers' lists, to note an article that was made of galvanized iron. The GI abbreviation eventually was taken to mean anything that was "government issue," and finally it came to stand for the soldiers themselves.

6 September

Received your letter at noon and must say it was the most beautiful letter I have ever had. Your big soldier's eyes were wet when he finished reading it. I wish I could tell you what it means to have someone who misses you, who is concerned with your troubles—who likes to hear the little trifles that happen throughout a long day. It's the richest thing a man could own.

About the war news, I feel as you do. I don't anticipate an immediate return home should the war in Europe end, but as you say, it could lift some restrictions and relieve a lot of our pain. It had better end suddenly, though, if I'm to stay in this country—and even that is questionable.

This P.M. we've been firing our rifles. I don't have the least interest, but merely go through the motions. With all that I'm amazed at my improvement. Last week I shot a perfect score with the M-1 rifle (standard 10-lb. rifle). It seems, with my disinterest, my quality improves—probably because I'm relaxed when firing, whereas in training, I was tense.

There are a few positive things in this camp. At Blanding, everything you did was scrutinized, as if we were babies. Here, with 400 guys shooting on this range, no one watches or raises the devil—yet the men do very well. There isn't someone always whipping us into the proper step; we talk in ranks everywhere we go, and our clothes are not examined through a "magnifying glass." These are the "pro" elements. I could tell you plenty of the "con," too.

Later—at the Service Club. I have a call in now, and will add a few lines if I get through to you.

Just spoke to you, Dearest, and it was wonderful. The time flew so fast. About the weekend, don't figure too heavily on it. I could be on detail, or I might not get the extra few hours that is needed to make it. If things work out, maybe there will be something to look forward to.

21 September, Happy Birthday, Neil!

As you know from the telephone call last night, I'm in Raleigh, No. Carolina. Came over to the USO [The

Combat training included practice under simulated warfare conditions, including gas attacks.

United Service Organizations, a volunteer civilian organization, provided recreational and social services to
members of the armed forces] chiefly to write you and
was pleasantly surprised they had a typewriter I could
use.

Before leaving camp yesterday I'd started a letter,
telling you that it would probably be the last uncensored

letter I could write. After Thursday, all mail will be censored from Fort Bragg. Of course I'm still hoping I don't leave with the Division after it reaches the P.O.E. [Port of Embarkation, the seaport from which a troopship departed for overseas.]

There seems so little to do in this city. I often think as I visit these towns and cities, even camps, how I'd enjoy them if you were with me. Army life has succeeded in teaching me something: that regardless how good—or terrible—something is, how it affects you is influenced by your attitude. "Attitude" is crammed down your neck and with good reason.

Right now I'm thinking of this interesting city, and I'm not enjoying it the way I could since I miss you so. But attitude is influenced by feeling and you can't turn off your feelings as easily as you do a faucet.

Neil is doing so much better. He seems to be developing into a strong little guy. Am glad you spent time with him on his subtraction. Once he catches on, he holds on to it. Since today is his birthday I bought 3 jerseys in a department store and had them mailed. Still looking for that wedding band I told you I was anxious to get for myself, but as yet haven't been satisfied.

> Men and women in the armed forces who were assigned the job of censor reviewed mail for classified or militarily sensitive information, which was then deleted. Americans working in factories producing war goods were also cautioned not to talk about what was being made because of the fear of enemy spies. Many posters reminded workers of the need for secrecy. One well-known poster displayed this message: Loose Lips Sink Ships.

23 September

Well, Honey, things have started to pop and at first glance you may not be too happy about it all. I know I wasn't. But first with the story—the pros and cons afterward.

First, there's little chance that I'll be leaving the Division, as I am now attached to the Medical Detachment of the 398th Infantry. Now, sit down—that was given to you a little fast.

It was very hard to swallow at first, but there are some good points, I've found. In the first place, I don't carry a rifle—no medics do, enemy or ally—because the terms of the Geneva Conference [the Geneva Conventions, see page 46] make such a provision. We wear a white band around our arm—and we're not supposed to get shot at. (I'm laughing.) This, at least, will eliminate our see-saw hopes and anticipation. It's all been settled for us—our concern about being transferred out of the Division, and if, or if not, I'll remain in the country. With the stroke of a pen they took care of it all very expeditiously—my future, our lives. Every soldier in the Army is manipulated like a puppet and you just have to take what's handed out.

One bright spot—the Lieutenant and Sergeant and boys are turning out to be really swell guys, and you can't begin to understand how much easier that makes it.

Dear, even now, for the love of me, I just can't see that we're going over—I really can't. My guess, which I emphasize is my opinion, is that we'll end up at the P.O.E. and stay there—at any rate, for quite a while.

It's ironical they put me in the Medical Detachment, without a single day of training. I spoke to the Lt. about my predicament—my reaction to blood, the whole bit. I assured him I wanted to cooperate to the best of my ability—go anywhere the Army sent me, but this would make me sick and I couldn't do the right job.

All he could say was that he sympathized with me, that he'd heard me talk with that Captain, and understood just how I felt—that he, too, was inclined to react that way—but what could he do? He said I'll have to learn to get used to it, that he knew it would be a hard dose to take, but could offer no encouragement.

It all seems so incredible and irrational. You see, if we were in combat and some poor guy was depending on my ability as a medic, which is nil, I don't feel capable of performing what would be expected of me. Also, my ineptness could mean a loss of life for some wounded soldier. Not only would I be incompetent, but the thought bugs me that I could be instrumental in the death of some boy or boys. It's so illogical—and typically Army thinking; they put you in a job you're not qualified for—yet your training and expertise in many other areas is completely disregarded. There are score of places I could be assigned, right here in the 398th Infantry where I could be an asset.

I will say that the boys have made this easier to take—a much better bunch than the rifle crowd. Don't write till you hear from me. From this point on—I'll probably call you.

I hope I haven't been crying on your shoulder too much, and that you don't feel too badly about it all. Perhaps things could be much worse. (At this moment it's hard to think of something!)

At least that awful suspense is over with—and I am happier here than in the other outfit. It's so comforting to know I have someone I can let my heart out to. I love you, Sweetheart.

Winston refers to the Geneva Conventions when he wrote to his wife about army medics not carrying weapons on the battlefield. The Geneva Conventions were accepted by all European countries, the United States, and some countries of Asia and South America. The provisions set standards for the humane treatment and care of wounded, shipwrecked, or sick military personnel—enemy or ally—and the treatment of prisoners of war. The protection of hospitals, med-

46

ical transports, and medical personnel marked with the red cross or a white band was also provided for by the Geneva Conventions.

27 September

As you are probably aware, things are happening—and fast. We have moved, but I can't tell you where although I think it permissible to say [censored].

We've all been promised passes and are counting the minutes till we get them, but am disappointed I'm not allowed to phone you.

Please don't be alarmed at all this secrecy, censoring and restrictions. You must realize it is for our protection. I assure you it's not nearly as bad as it sounds; it's just that the Army goes all out to keep secret the movements and whereabouts of this organization. They don't put us in a cage, I assure you, as we're given unlimited privileges, i.e., passes.

You're probably anxious to hear more about my transfer to the Medical Corps. And as I said before, aside from my reaction to blood, which is the least of it—but this reaction might be the cause of a loss of life, and my conscience would never be clear. I still can't understand the rationale behind the transfer to this branch since the officers responsible were aware of all this—and it was repeated to 4 different echelons.

However, since the boys here, the non-coms and Lieutenant are very easy to get along with, I wouldn't mind staying with the Medical Corps—if only in a capacity that would not put me in constant contact with the wounded.

I find it difficult to write you, knowing my letter is being censored—and also knowing how you like to hear of my activities in detail. But censor or not, I know I can tell you how much I miss you and Neil and David. Have you tried feeding David ice-cream again? Isn't it odd he shows so little interest in it, whereas Neil liked it so much at his age. I ache so much to see him. I was thinking of the recent weekend I came home—how David, so early in the morning, joined happily in on the family reunion.

Someone in the barracks has a radio and I just learned today is Yom Kippur [a solemn Jewish holy day—the Day of Atonement]. It didn't have too much of an effect on me until I noticed, while Jewish music and observances were coming from the radio, that the boy below my bunk was crying and reading his prayer book, and for his head covering, he used his helmet. It moved me deeply.

By now you must realize if I've neglected to write certain things—and I know there's an important explanation you're looking for—it's because I'm not permitted to write about it. But if I say everything is okay—it could be a lot worse.

Miss you terribly—and it's not too impossible that you may get a surprise soon. Note new address:

Pvt. Keith Winston 33927775
2nd Bn. Hq. Co. 398th Inf. APO 447
c/o Postmaster, New York, N.Y.

I'm sure you're writing, but because of my change of address I've not been getting any mail—nor has anyone else.

We've been promised passes, and the anticipation, the worry that I'll be eligible for one is making a nervous wreck of me. To be with you will mean more than anything in this world. I feel like a balloon growing bigger and bigger, almost ready to burst at the slightest provocation.

Last night I took a walk around the camp. It made me feel considerably better, although the "balloon" feeling still persists. Don't have an awful lot to say, since what I'd like to say isn't permitted. I'm always thinking of you, Sweetheart. Kiss the boys for me. I want you to know you're forever on my mind. At the risk of sounding corny, keep the "home fires" burning—I feel certain everything will be okay soon.

48

3

ATLANTIC OCEAN

OCTOBER 1944

At Sea

I received your letter, written after you were convinced I was going over, and your reactions were identical to mine. You know, Dear, I never realized that my family would be the only thing on my mind when leaving. I knew it would be uppermost, but surely I felt I'd be thinking of the boat ride: would I be seasick, where in God's world were we headed, would I ever come back. And once on the boat I was sure I'd be constantly worrying about the crossing hazards—the subs and mines.

But strangely enough none of that seems to bother me—in fact I'm hardly concerned.

The only think I can think of now is that every day and every mile on this boat takes me farther and farther away from you and our boys.

On the day we were leaving I don't think any of us realized the significance of it too much. We all seemed to be rather numbed by the final turn of things. It was

Keith Winston, with his sons Neil and David, during his home leave before being shipped overseas.

weird—not until retreat, when the National Anthem was being played did the actual impact hit me, and I realized I was leaving my homeland, and that this would be the last time I would hear it—for a long time—on native soil. And for the first time I know well what the Star-Spangled Banner meant to one who was leaving his country. And it hit hard.

Another thing that touched me deeply was the warm way the Red Cross handled us as we were ready to march up that gangplank. What a wonderful feeling to know that somebody cared—even a stranger—and was on hand to say good-bye. Besides the liberal refreshments, each of us was given a large pouch with a number of useful things in it.

It was good that we had discussed the probability of my leaving when I was last home. And the clue that I would give you if I couldn't call you, so I was pretty certain you would "see through" the bouquet of roses I wired home. I felt so damn helpless, being so close, yet unable to talk to you. But as I think back, maybe I would rather have said good-bye as we did—I shall never forget you as you stood outside the train window. You were so beautiful, so refreshing a sight, and such a pleasant thought to look back at.

We haven't learned where we're headed for—officially—although I'm sure it is the [censored] theater, if my deduction is correct as to the way the ship is headed in relation to the sun.

By the time you get this letter you will know, I'm sure, since this letter won't be mailed till we reach our destination, and I'll probably have others to go along with it then.

I've had a case of seasickness all the way, so far, although somewhat relieved this afternoon. If I write few letters on this trip you'll know why.

The above was written the 2nd day; and from then

on until this writing I've been seasick. Now that I'm feeling better, and I assure you I am, I'll get back to writing you.

There's absolutely nothing to do on ship. We sit on deck when and if we find the room—no comforts whatsoever. If I'm not talking with someone I'm thinking of you and the children, and yearn and yearn and yearn, and as I realize the ship is taking me farther away from you, it becomes unbearable. I've read your letter over a number of times—the one I received on the ship—and being the only real "home touch" I have among my possessions, it means so much to me. While I'm thinking of it, mail me copies of those two pictures I like so much of the three of you.

Lots of things are happening here that I can't talk about, but have made indelible impressions on me, so rather than forget about them, I'm jotting down a few things—my impressions, etc. that someday we can read together.

Jim is not on the boat but I will no doubt see him at the destination, which we already know, but still not permitted to reveal. I plan to cable, if allowed, as soon as I arrive.

There seems to be some argument as to whether airmail or V-Mail is better. Of course, you can't enclose anything with V-Mail, and must use the prescribed envelope. Also, it takes extra time to photograph V-Mail. So the consensus is that airmail is faster. I'm going to mail a V-Mail letter—marking it #1, just as I have this letter—and take special note of the difference in receipt.

For the time being, mail airmail, getting the $.06 airmail envelope. If you don't have one handy, just put the same postage on and in large print add OVERSEAS AIR MAIL. Also, rather than wait for the mailman to pick it up, put it in the mailbox immediately as a delay of one pick-up could mean a delay of a week, more or less.

V-Mail was a system for transmitting letters that was designed to save space on the transport ships and planes crossing back and forth from the United States to the war zones. The procedure was simple: letters to or from soldiers and sailors were written on special V-Mail stationery, photographed and reproduced on microfilm. The film was mailed to its destination, enlarged and printed, and delivered. Unfortunately, photos and other objects could not be included in V-Mail letters, but the writer could draw pictures. The letter V stood for Victory. You can see one of Keith Winston's V-Mail letters on page 66.

Another day

Perhaps the little I'm permitted to say about the boat ride may be of interest. First, while we only eat two meals a day, they're pretty substantial. It seems cooking goes on all the time as there's always an odor of food. Now that I'm over being seasick, I don't mind it too much.

In the "holes"—the troops' quarters—it's disgustingly sickening, since air is lacking and it's so crowded you can't move without bumping into some soldier. All this makes it hot and putrid smelling since we have such poor facilities for bathing—and the clothes STINK.

From what I can see, the small percentage of officers on board have as much room as the combined troops. I have not seen one solitary chair where an enlisted man can sit down to write a letter. He sits on deck or his bunk to write. I tell you this since it's about over and you need not worry—but it has aroused a resentful feeling, not only within me, but in everyone around me. I wonder if things like this come under the heading of military discipline (officers are not to mingle with enlisted men—to instill respect and dignity). If this is so—that thinking is way off base as it has created the exact opposite effect, a complete lack of respect for the officers and the System.

I could say much more, but what's the use. It doesn't bring us any closer (in spirit), and to me that is the main purpose of our letters.

This letter is extended because I have been adding a little more to it each day and all will be mailed at once on arrival at destination. Never doubt for one second that you are always on my mind—I love you.

INTO
COMBAT
OCTOBER TO DECEMBER 1944

The 100th Division arrived in Marseilles, France, on October 20, 1944, so the letter that follows was misdated. At this time the 100th Division became part of the U.S. Seventh Army. Their assignment was to relieve veteran troops of the 45th Infantry Division and join in the attack on the German positions in the Vosges Mountains. During this period Winston received his transfer from the 2nd to the 3rd Battalion medics.

19 October 1944, France—V-Letter #1

We are here at last. Where I am, and what I am doing, and what I have seen—I cannot say—but it has been a revelation.

I have always said how much I appreciated my wife and children and home and community and American way of living. Today I saw it again, but my appreciation comes from a fuller realization of what it all means. Seeing

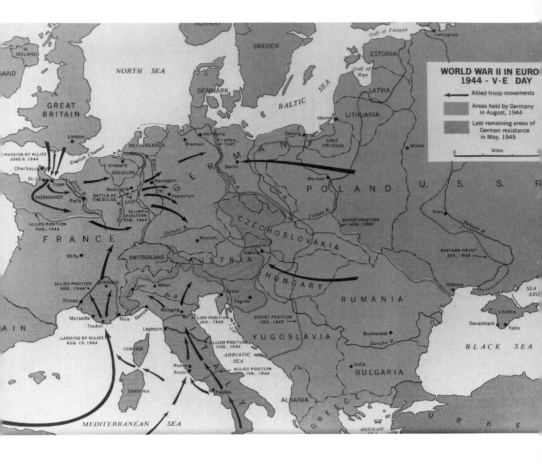

boys, as young as our little Neil, begging for money or something to eat. Tears come to my eyes, at first in pity and compassion for a world so torn up and terrible that it could reduce itself to such horror—then in thankfulness that our boys would never have to resort to this because we live in America—because we happen to be fortunate enough to be living in America.

God has been good to us. Don't feel too badly that we're being asked to give up just a little of our happiness, temporarily, so that other people just like us who are not Americans, can have a taste of what we're having.

We haven't been told yet how much we can say in our letters home, but I'm playing it safe and saying little regarding location. I hope Neil and David are well. However brief, I'll do my utmost to get a letter off to you daily.

My deepest love.

24 October

It gets dark so quickly here, my Dearest, and sometimes you start a letter and find it impossible to complete. There is no light (electric, etc.), after darkness sets in. We live in tents, bivouac style. I don't enjoy it—nobody does—but once over here, with all the discomfort you see among civilians you realize that all this is part of accomplishing our ultimate goal.

We've had so much rain, rain and more rain, and French mud is really mud. Our shoes and leggings are always muddy, but our tents are dry and that means everything.

My Sweetheart, I'd go through all this every day for the rest of my life if it meant being with you. My only real discomfort, my only real heartache is being away from you. But then I start to rationalize—we could be in the States, in a camp like the IRTC [Infantry Ranger Training Center, such as Fort Benning, Georgia] and I'd be unable to see you for 5 or 6 months anyway, and maybe it won't be more than that, maybe less, in this situation. Keep yourself busy, it helps so much.

My tent mate is a young boy from Springfield, Mass. While only 23, he's been around—looks much older. Unlike the average GI he tries to be so considerate, and I sure appreciate that. At present I'm involved in a "Mr. Anthony" dilemma. He's been married 3 months—after knowing his wife only one week, and has been with her one month out of the three. She's Protestant, he's Jewish, and like most newly married couples trying to adjust themselves, have innumerable arguments. These continued through the mail, and her last letter suggested divorce. Naturally, he was terribly upset at the thought of losing her, for he does love her—and at my suggestion, which he solicited, wrote her a beautiful love letter. He said I made him feel so much better. So now, I'm watching the outcome with much interest.

Mr. Anthony was a popular radio program of the 1940s. Listeners with problems called to ask advice from Mr. Anthony. Most of the problems had to do with romance or heartaches. Radio and television call-in talk shows today are very similar, as are Dear Abby and Ann Landers newspaper advice columns.

Don't send any money since we use French currency, and will have no use for it. And by the time I'd get it, I'd be paid for October. You might send me a few blank checks though, as I might want to send for something in the States. You probably already know the regulations concerning packages being sent overseas.

There are a few things I could use—candy, nuts, plenty of it, but make sure they're packed in cans. Perhaps once a week, but I'll have to write a written request each time—these are the rules. Also a jackknife and a few bars of soap. Cookies, too, the kind that don't crumble and get any worse with age—and a plum pudding from Horn & Hardart's would be welcome. Call P.O. to learn exact size and regulations. We're outdoors all day and I get very hungry—often eating C and K rations.

The villagers are interesting here. Cigarettes are practically nil, and they'll barter almost anything for them. They have plenty of wine, and that is their chief source of exchange. Since I don't go for wine much, I've traded for grapes and pears, which are delicious—the only food items there's no scarcity of. A franc is only worth $.02 in American currency—used to be about $.19.

Even with trading and bartering, Keith Winston probably needed money from home from time to time as the average enlisted member of the military received only $50.00 a month. Today, a recruit with less than four months' service receives $770 a month. The money is automatically deposited to his or her bank account to lessen the likelihood of it being spent all at once.

25 October

Today received your first letter—first V-Mail! It's been a long time en route, so in the future use only airmail.

We're not working too hard, and our little Medical Group is turning out to be quite friendly. The Captain and Lt. are decent, democratic guys, and pleasant, and don't go around pulling rank. When work comes up it's shared cooperatively. Much happier here than in the Infantry.

Don't expect a letter from me daily, Dearest, even though I write, as the mail doesn't leave each day, so you'll probably be receiving a few at a time. I'll try to number my letters as you do so you can read them in proper sequence.

26 October

Today your 4 V-Mail letters made me a very happy man. As yet no regular mail, which is due by boat. However, I'm relieved and happy now that mail has started coming in.

On pass, today, we spent time in the large city near our bivouac area—intensely interesting. Wish I could tell you the name of it. The French are a unique breed.

Bargaining is the rule, not the exception. There are no places to eat—not even refreshments, except for drinks or grapes or pears. Rumor has it that the Army will allow us an extra C or K ration to compensate for the meal we miss on pass.

Just got back from town where I'd been writing this letter in the Red Cross Club. It was a treat to be indoors for a change—the first time since getting off the boat a week ago. A number of American women direct the Club, although the help are French. It's no cinch for a woman to be here and they're much appreciated.

Saw a wedding band I liked in a window; it was after store hours but I expect to go back in a couple of days and purchase it. It will be a constant reminder of our solid union.

30 October, En route

Now that we're on the move I can give you a few details of our trip not permitted earlier, as every move is secret. Now that we've left, I can tell you the "big city" I kept mentioning was Marseilles. We landed there October 20th after a long, miserable 15-day voyage.

We sailed through the Gibraltar Strait, getting a good view of the famous Rock. North Africa lay to our right, and Spain to our left as we coursed through the 22-mile-long, 8-mile-wide straits. Despite the distance of 8 miles, the two coasts were surprisingly visible. We sailed 2 days on the Mediterranean Sea which was like glass—glistening, warm, beautiful. But late in the second day we ran into a raging Mediterranean storm and went through a night I shall never forget.

We docked in Marseilles, a city about the size of Baltimore. Effects of bombing were visible in some areas but in the main sections you'd hardly know it was a war city, except for the constant presence of soldiers—Allied soldiers from all over the world. Wine is the chief industry, and with U.S. cigarettes the boys are stocking up plenty. After dark the city suddenly becomes quiet and by 9 P.M. the streets are clear of American soldiers.

As Keith Winston was serving in the Army, his letters deal with that branch of the service. However, a word needs to be said about the other branches that helped achieve victory in WWII. The Army Air Force, created in 1941, had 2.4 million members by the end of the war. The Navy had over 3 million members by 1945. The Marine Corps, a part of the Navy, was a specialized combat service. By 1945 there were 474,680 marines in service. The Coast Guard patrolled Greenland, staffed Navy transports, and conducted amphibious landings and rescues. At the height of the war over 106,000 people were serving in the Coast Guard. Civilians made up the Merchant Marine, which assisted the Navy in transporting troops and cargo. In the peak war years, more than 250,000 people took part in this dangerous work. By 1942 all the armed forces permitted women to serve in support roles but not in combat. Women served as typists, drivers, photographers, mechanics, and transport plane pilots. The Women's Army Auxiliary Corps (WAAC) was established in 1942, and by 1945, there were 99,000 women in uniform. Because of the shortage of personnel, women were also recruited to fly cargo aircraft. Licensed female pilots flew in the Women's Auxiliary Ferrying Squadron (WAFS), and new pilots were trained in the Women's Flying Training Detachment. In 1943 the two groups were joined and became the Women's Airforce Service Pilots—WASPs. As many as 1,072 WASPs flew more than 60 million miles in every aircraft used at the time. Women who joined the

Navy were called WAVES—Women Accepted for Volunteer Emergency Service. Women were accepted in the Marine Corps in 1943, and eventually 19,000 women served in this branch. Women in the Coast Guard were called SPARs (Semper Paratus—Always Ready). More than 10,000 women were inducted into the Coast Guard.

4 November

Church bells were ringing when I awoke this morning and for a split second became excited and full of anticipation, half-dreaming half-hoping it could mean the cessation of hostilities. Somehow I feel the war could end just that simply and suddenly. The Stars & Stripes, the Army newspaper, was supposed to arrive daily but we haven't seen one yet; consequently we know nothing about what is happening. The one thing we do know, however, is that the European War is still very much on, and right now all other news is secondary.

Censorship is pretty strict and I can't tell you of my whereabouts. However, I'm willing to bet our location was already published in U.S. papers. Read the papers carefully and you'll probably find out where we are before you find out from me. You remember our Division—I can't mention it here, nor should you when you write. Don't hesitate to let me know anything you learn about us—and I'm not kidding.

10 November

Today I heard our President was re-elected. I know you're pleased—and that goes double for me.

My new set-up, though very temporary, is exceptionally comfortable, especially after having lived in tents up until now. The small group of medics are actually living in a house—plenty of warmth, food, and a chance to shave with warm water.

A photograph taken during the Normandy invasion shows how quickly medical corps personnel provided treatment. Here, just a few feet ashore, a soldier wounded during the landing was given a plasma transfusion.

Conditions don't permit me to write a longer letter, but I'm well, comfortable and hopeful. I pray daily for an abrupt ending and that I'll soon get home and be able to put my arms around you.

11 November

Today is Armistice Day [a day named to commemorate November 11, 1918, when at 11 A.M. World War I combattants laid down their arms, marking the end of a terrible war] and I couldn't help thinking what it must have meant 26 years ago when we thought we fought a war to "end all wars"—and all the attending lunacy of war. And that people, once and for all, had had their fill, and realized the futility of greed and senseless killing. And that finally we'd seen the last of wars. But the world didn't count on the insanity of power-mad "leaders" who could throw civilization back a century or more—and that our so-called civilization would have lost its meaning, and make you wonder what this world's about anyway. And though I'm not a praying guy as you know, I did pray today, hoping for a complete rout and defeat of these madmen, and that we'd know peace again before it's too late for us and our children. It's hard to believe, Honey, but power-hungry lunatics are around in all countries, including our own—and my outlook isn't too bright for a peaceful world 26 years from now. People in our country don't begin to know the meaning of war—and don't care—until it hits them; when one of their family is killed or wounded.

Re: your letter in which you ask me to confirm or disaffirm certain presumptions. All I can do is refer you to the newspaper, if and when they print it. I can't say anything—yet. It sounds ridiculous but the censorship is usually lifted through Washington, and the newspapers print it the same day. By the time we're told, it's another two weeks. Then 10 days by mail to you.

Neil and his good work in school continues to be a source of great pleasure. And David's doings delight me. I love them both so much. Darling, I'm so tired. The main thing is that I'm well. Take care of yourself and the children.

14 November, Somewhere in France

Was transferred to Hq. Co. [Headquarter's Company] from the 2nd Bn. My new address will be as the envelope states—Medical Detachment—instead of 2nd Bn. Hq. Co. I haven't heard from you for a few days, and now with the change of address, it may take a few days before mail catches up. Your letters are my mainstay. I'm still waiting anxiously for the pictures.

While I have little faith in the rumor, I hear Gen. Patton says he'll be in Berlin before December.

Darling, I'm so homesick. Praying, hoping, writing just don't seem to satisfy. The feeling is worse sometimes more than others but I'll snap out of it. Today I'm laid low with it but please don't let it bother you too much, and know that when you read this I'll be over it.

Harry—the boy from Boston—is in this section and I'll probably be seeing a lot of him. It will give me a lift.

Winston doesn't give Harry's last name. Harry and Winston became friends when they served together in a rifle unit during combat training. Winston writes only that Harry was 29, unmarried, a graduate of Boston University, a native of Boston and a very likable character.

Just heard something new—that I'm to be transferred to the 3rd Bn. Hq. Medical Section—but write to the same address until I tell you otherwise. You're forever in my heart—and I'll never be happy till I can hold you in my arms again.

23 November
Dear Sonny Boy, [Winston's son Neil.]

Today is Thanksgiving Day. I guess you and Mother and David will have turkey or chicken. I hope so. I'm sure next Thanksgiving will be different. Right now, let's plan

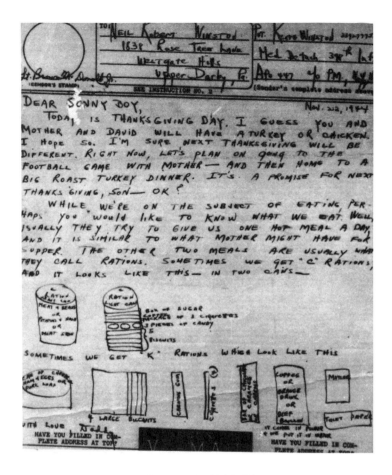

Keith Winston's V-Mail letter

on going to the football game with Mother—and then home to a big roast turkey dinner. It's a promise for next Thanksgiving, Son—OK?

While we're on the subject of eating, perhaps you would like to know what we eat. Well, usually they try to give us one hot meal a day, and it is similar to what

Mother might have for supper. The other two meals are usually what they call rations. Sometimes, we get "C" rations, and it looks like this—in two cans—

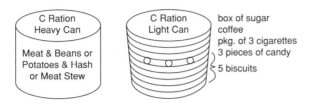

Sometimes we get "K" rations which look like this:

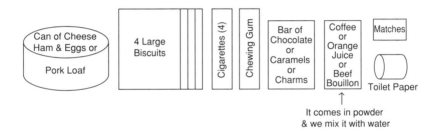

With love, Daddy

28 November

Have been on the move again and missed your letter. This town has turned out to be interesting for me. I ran into a civilian, a man about 30, married, with a 5-year-old daughter, who speaks English, and he's done everything possible to make things comfortable for me. Through his generosity I slept on a feather mattress, and enjoyed a few home-cooked meals for a change. I like to think it was reciprocal. My presence gave him a chance to learn things about America he was eager to know. And my offering them little things like soap, cigarettes, bouillon, cheese, candy, etc. was helpful to them.

He works in an office and seemed like quite a capable individual. Showed me a picture-frame holder he devised from the waste of a product his firm manufactures, and they paid him handsomely for his idea. He owns a large "wireless" (radio), something uncommon here. They played the Victrola [record player] last night and made a real effort to be hospitable.

It's remarkable how well the French make out with the little food they have. His wife, who can't speak English, made soup from potatoes which was exceptionally good. Then for the main dish—potatoes and hot dogs from a can of GI hot dogs a Captain gave them a few days earlier—and pudding and tea. Of course, under these conditions, I ate very sparingly. He told me food is difficult to get but day by day he manages to get satisfactory amounts. It's far from good, he says, but they can get by. For instance, butter is next to impossible to buy unless you pay $8 a lb. at the black market, even though the "ceiling" price is $.70 (equivalent in U.S. money).

He was amazed to know we could get 2 pairs of shoes annually and all the clothing we could buy. Everything here is rationed, and half the time the ration points are worthless since there's no food or commodities. The town itself is a typical European village—probably the size of our Westgate, but old and rustic. I know you would love the quiet beauty of the place. It has 2 or 3 beer taverns—a principal European commodity—and a bakery still in operation. Other than that, no business places. It's close to a rather large city where most purchasing is done.

Well, at last five letters arrived! Hope I'll be hearing more regularly now. We're still in the beautiful village, and the feather mattress was again slept on last night, this time shared with Harry. I went down to his Co. to get him since I know that he, coming from a rifle Co., never gets a chance to sleep indoors. He said it was like heaven and thanked me a thousand times. We enjoyed another evening with these French people and have hopes of spending another night there.

Was happy you voted [in the presidential election of 1944] and pleased that your enthusiasm matches mine. These French people I stayed with told us that the Germans, for 3 months, were telling them Roosevelt couldn't make it, and Dewey [Republican candidate, Thomas E. Dewey] was sure to be elected—they were emphatic. I share your delight in Roosevelt's victory and the defeat of those reactionary congressmen.

29 November

Am having a hey-day with the mail situation. Five letters yesterday, 3 today, and a chance of more coming. Do I have to tell you how I feel? I'm very sorry my mail isn't coming through as it should, but eventually you'll get it. Remember—first, I must find the time to write, then the censor must find the time to censor, then mail must be sent back to the A.P.O. This could make for a 3- or 4-day delay.

As to what I sleep on in the tent. We cover the ground with pine needles when available, then 2 blankets, with 4 to cover us (2 men in tent). I assure you it isn't like home but after a while it becomes easier to accept. However, being a Medic, I—perhaps 35% of the time—am in a house—even if it means sleeping on the floor. And the important thing is that it's dry.

Tonight I have a steak dinner awaiting—with apple pie. Harry suggested we ask the French family to cook a steak dinner if we provide the steak, and they were delighted. We traded cigarettes for steak—and 7 P.M. we eat—and then a feather bed to sleep in—ahem!

Rumors run thick and fast there are peace negotiations with Gen. Eisenhower, and that the President is in Paris.

with the family love ...

Bizet family Apr. 6
Beauvais, France 1945

PASSED BY 37261 U S ARMY EXAMINER

2 December

There is something I should tell you, Darling. About the 1st of November, one of our boys stepped on a shoe mine. He was definitely where he was ordered not to be. Even though this was far behind the lines, it takes some time for our engineers to clear mine fields. This boy was hurt and required a stretcher and 4 men to bring him in. I was one of the four chosen to get him. As we started out, one of the four litter bearers stepped on another mine and was badly injured. The concussion cut my lip and it bled rather badly. My C.O. [Commanding Officer], trying to be a good fellow, recommended me for the Purple Heart medal. I really thought it was a gag as this was minor to what I'd been seeing all about me. For that reason, said nothing to you. But it wasn't a gag, and yesterday the Regiment Colonel gave me the medal. It's nothing to be proud of, and I'm only sending it to you for its souvenir value. Now I don't want you getting the idea my job is so dangerous. A thing like this occurs rarely.

Apparently, Winston made light of his injury in order to spare his wife Sarah worry. However, his wound was far worse than a cut lip. His Purple Heart citation reads: "During this lengthy period of combat oper-

Letters sent home sometimes included a photograph, and these too had to be passed by the censor (see reverse of top photo): Cpl. Jack McKeever with local friends in Beauvais, France; WAVE Alma Klein Walensky, Sp3c [specialist third class]; Edgar Schlossberg, PO3c [petty officer third class], aviation machinist's mate, seen here at home on leave; Staff Sgt. John Albert Armistead.

The Purple Heart was awarded to soldiers wounded or killed in battle.

ations against the enemy, PFC Keith Winston, medical technician, displayed rare courage, technical skill and devotion to duty in carrying out his daily duties. Participating in the bitter campaign for the Vosges Mountains in Alsace-Lorraine, penetration of the Maginot defenses near the fortress of Bitche, and the push into Germany proper, PFC Winston risked his life on innumerable occasions so that wounded soldiers could be given the proper attention. On November 8, 1944, Winston, when trying to rescue a wounded soldier in a mine field, was wounded himself."

3 December

Today—another day—and hopefully one day closer to victory and you. At present we're located in a big hotel "sans" Bellevue Stratford [an elegant Philadelphia hotel of the period] service, of course! But it's dry and we're making use of the stoves in every room.

Sent off the medal. Please say nothing to anyone about it. One reason, too, that I mentioned it was that you might see my name listed in the paper and really get upset over it. Again I say I'm perfectly well—no ill effects whatsoever. Actually, my first impulse was to throw it away, but it really is an attractive thing and I changed my mind.

The Army is catching up on cigarette and chocolate rations. You see, we're supposed to get 1 pack a day, as well as a small bar of chocolate and stick of gum. Being on the move so much the rations are often missed but they keep accumulating. So in the last 5 days we've received innumerable packs of cigarettes, bars of chocolates, gum, shaving cream, tooth powder, toothbrushes, etc.—more than we can use. Knowing of the cigarette shortage back home, the boys joke about sending them back to the States.

5 December

I know it would be foolish to tell you there is absolutely no danger involved—but, Dearest, there is an inherent danger in just about every move you make in life—even in peacetime. But we try to do the best we can. So please accept all this, as I'm doing—not only will it make you feel better, but it will make me feel much better, too. Okay?

You must be wondering, and perhaps concerned about my first assignment up front. Well, here it is: Our team was rushed out to pick up a seriously injured boy. To be more explicit—to pick up a boy whose leg was blown off. You can imagine my reaction at the thought. But this was my job, and I was in the Army and I had no alternative but to go. However, as we got closer, I was determined to avoid looking at this catastrophe, and tried to keep my head averted as much as it was possible. But somehow—and this is really uncanny—the first thing that drew my eyes, as if magnetized, was his torn-off leg. I was almost in a state of shock, and I just stood there, staring, almost not believing what I saw. But, Honey, somehow a super strength rushes through in moments like these—and I was aware that the life of this boy depended on our immediate and careful attention. To make a long, gruesome story short, I did what I was sent out to do—and that was my first and thorough initiation. After that, I was about ready for anything.

I'm pretty tired now and this candlelight doesn't make for easy writing. Goodnight—until later.

7 December

Today is the 3rd anniversary of U.S. involvement in the war and I pinned some hope on that date for the war to be over, but the day is still here, and the war is still on. Maybe something will turn up to answer my—and millions of others'—prayers.

I miss so much the daily newspapers and magazines. As you know we have no way of keeping up with home news, or even war news, except for Stars & Stripes and that paper is not much more than a school paper—nothing really newsworthy.

Medics delivered first aid in the battle zone.

Though I find the native people interesting, I have a heck of time making myself understood. You can't realize that language can be such an important factor in mixing with people. You know, someday I'd like to see a universal language taught in every school in every country, along with the native language. Then all language barriers would disappear—no matter where you might go. The way I feel now, though, once I get back on American soil, I'll probably never want to leave again.

11 December

We're married 12½ years today—half of a silver anniversary. Happy half-anniversary, Dearest! I have a feeling that these next years are going to be real happy ones—with lots of activity centered around Home Sweet Home—seeing our children grow up, improving our little home, and most of all, always remembering to appreciate the little things in life. Agree?

Well, today I was transferred back to my old section—2nd Bn. Hq. They welcomed me very enthusiastically and it really gave me a lift. I'm tickled to be back with them.

I bumped into Henry, the boy who married his wife after a week's courtship. Didn't have a chance to talk much so I don't know what happened yet, but will soon.

13 December

Yesterday we set up quarters in a tremendous French home—really magnificent. It was owned by an American. There's a powerful radio that receives stations from every county in the world—and clearly, too.

We listen to the news whenever we can, and we must have heard the same news a dozen times—probably like you do at home. And all along the front the news was cheering the day that 2,400 planes in one group bombed important industrial plants in Frankfurt. I just can't see how Germany holds out with all their reversals. She may pass out completely any day now.

Again we moved last night and are quartered in a picturesque little stone home (they're all stone in France) with 4 rooms—all on one floor, similar to the $3,990 homes we see in the States.

Well, well, well. I've just been handed 2 pieces of the stuff that keeps me going and how I did enjoy them!

Now I can talk a little more freely about my Division—within bounds, however, as censorship is still very much with us.

We're in the Alsace-Lorraine section of France, where the German language is spoken considerably more than French, and in the last 4 years the people have lived under German jurisdiction. Their sympathies are not too well defined—neither Nazi nor Ally, though some are strongly pro-Ally, and others pro-Nazi. These are the quiet, silent ones and you don't have to be too smart to see where their allegiance lies—Germans at heart, with hidden swastikas showing up at the wrong moment, as well as their pro-Nazi periodicals.

They drink ersatz [a substitute made of inferior ingredients] coffee and much of the food is synthetic.

One thing they welcome from us is white bread. They only have the "black bread," comparable to our pumpernickel, and when fresh we enjoy it very much. To them, white bread is almost like cake. They can vegetables and store plenty of apples and potatoes. When they need meat, a cow is slaughtered. They have hordes of marks [German currency], but as I said, have little or nothing to buy. I enclosed one for Neil.

As to the Army I'm in—it's the 7th Army under General Patch, not the 3rd as you thought. General Patch has a reputation for being exceptionally thoughtful of the men under his command—and from my vantage point, has proven it.

Speaking of the Alsatian sympathies, I have seen many families with two sons—one in the German army and the other in the French army. They seem to be indifferent to principles—they're just sick of war.

5

COUNTER-ATTACKING

DECEMBER 1944 TO MARCH 1945

31 December

You ask about my duties. By this time you probably already know—but if you're still in question—I'm the Bn. Aide Station clerk. It's just the type of work I like and am trained for. I'm also called a technician—which means I help in dispensing medicines and care for sick boys who need attention. I have lots to learn, but know of no better place to learn F-A-S-T.

If you please—in the future you will address me as Private First Class. I have been "promoted." As to the injury—I assure you I'm okay. No scars—well, and happy as could be expected.

5 January

Received your two V-Mail letters at once and it was interesting to compare your own words about the war. In your first, you spoke discouragingly about the war. You felt it wouldn't end until spring. Then the next day when the Germans' advance was completely squashed, you felt the war could end this winter. I'm the same way. It's an up and down see-saw, isn't it? Continue to give me your views as I know they're formed after listening to many commentators—and I'm far from informed about the whole front. I'm still restricted in what I say. I hope you're getting more news on the 7th Army front by now.

If people back home realized the importance of donating blood (through the Red Cross), a lot more would be forthcoming. I've seen with my own eyes what blood plasma does for a wounded boy. If only the world could see a sick, injured boy hovering around death, then when blood plasma is administered, see color return to his face, see him smile with hope—more people would make it their duty to give blood. Today a boy came in in pretty bad shape, but by the time he left you wouldn't believe the improvement unless you saw it yourself. I felt so good to know that I might have been instrumental in an infinitesimal part of his revival. I'm always on hand to help the doctor.

Keith mentions the American Red Cross in several of his letters to his family. He knew about the Red Cross collection of blood plasma, which began in 1941 as war was just starting to threaten the United States. During the peak war years of 1944 and 1945, more than 7.5 million people volunteered to work for the Red Cross on the homefront and in camp activities such as shipping food and medicine parcels. The Red Cross also taught safety and nutrition courses, and helped hospitals when they were short-staffed. Over 13 million units of blood were collected by the Red Cross and 70,000 of its registered nurses served with the military. Occasionally, in other letters, Winston complains about the American Red Cross. Like other GIs, he felt the Red Cross should have offered services that the Army did not provide. For example, he would have liked them to offer writing paper and

Red Cross workers serving in combat areas lived in conditions very similar to those the GIs endured.

envelopes, and thought they should supply magazines and newspapers, too.

10 January

Things are happening and we're busy. I may not be able to write as regularly as I'd like. I'm sure you get the picture.

We've been having a little radio trouble. However, our resourceful medics have procured telephone receiving equipment and a loudspeaker, and with a few ingenious machinations, most of our station personnel hear programs.

Our telephone set-up is great. The amazing thing about our organization, regardless if it's Bn., Regiment or Division, if all or any part moves—anywhere—a telephone hook-up is working within an hour after arriving at our destination. All the Companies, Medics, Headquarters are connected by wire. And it's really quite simple, too. I plan to make use of hook-ups throughout the house once I get back and equipment is available.

You ask me to describe the men I work with. In our outfit we have a physician (C.O.) who is Captain, as you know. We call him "Doc." Then we have a Lieutenant who takes care of the administrative end. He's a tall, slim guy about 6' 4½" and was only attached to us recently. He saw service in Africa, Anzio, Italy, and now France. When relating his experiences he often says "beaucoup" soldiers, "beaucoup" jeeps, "beaucoup" this and that, meaning "much" in French. Now, everyone calls him "Beaucoup" since that's a perfect description of his height. He's a funny guy and does a lot for morale around here.

We're running into a lot of German-speaking people now—and with a little knowledge of Yiddish and German, we are gradually learning to understand them. A favorite expression of ours is "nix fushtay" [a garbled blend of Yiddish and slang, meaning "I don't understand"]. And when they say something that may not be favorable, even though we know what they're saying, we smile and say, "nix fushtay." This is exactly what they say, too, when they don't want to understand us.

14 January

The Russian advance has been real encouragement, and it may be the beginning of the end of our enemy.

Want to hear something funny? Right now the boys

82

are talking about the fun they had at Ft. Bragg. It was pretty tough down there but now it seems like a country club in comparison.

You might like to know how we sleep. We use a sleeping bag which with the extra insert is equivalent to 4 blankets. It zips up to the face and leaves a little opening around the mouth and nose about the size of a grapefruit in diameter. It's very warm and I like it. When zipped up we look like mummies.

We're always running into new experiences. Right now it seems we're treating more civilians than GIs. These little towns have no doctors and when one shows up they besiege him. We get eggs, liquor and thanks in return. Today a 2-month-old baby was brought in. With no vitamins or cereals to prescribe, Doc hardly knew what to suggest. A change in diet would have helped the baby but all they have here is milk (for an infant).

The boys talk of visiting Paris which is some distance away. If the war did end abruptly, could you picture a few million GIs with the same thought converging on the city. Can you imagine the result? Until later, Darling.

19 January

Suddenly we got "busy" and this is the first chance I grabbed to write. It has been snowing continuously. Last night, not only was it snowy, but pitch black. So dark, you couldn't see your hand in front of you. Literally.

Doc asked me to cross the street—where the Sgt. is staying—to pick up some supplies. Well, I tried and tried but it was so black outside, despite the snow, I couldn't find the house—not to mention slipping on the ice and walking headlong into a manure pile. (I'll tell you more about manure pile later.) When I came back empty-handed the boys laughed. So another guy tried—one who said it was a cinch—and he too returned with no results. So, smugly confident, the Captain said, "I'll go." And the four of us bet him 200 francs that he couldn't find the place

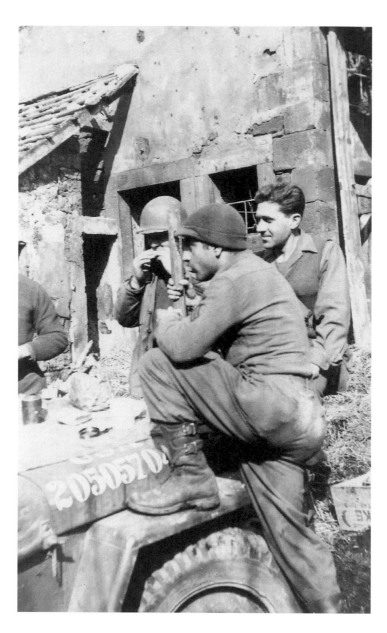

*Keith Winston (bare-headed) in a
combat area in France*

either in half an hour, even though it was just across the street.

Well, for twenty minutes he was out there trying with no better results. But luck was with the doctor, for suddenly a gigantic flare (lights used by troops) lit up the sky brilliantly for about 3 minutes—and looking out the door we saw Doc running like the devil to that house. He found it, but we tell him he had to pull "rank" to accomplish his mission, by calling the line troops to furnish a flare. It cost each of us 50 francs but we got some fun out of it.

About the manure piles. Over here a civilian's wealth is measured by the height of his manure pile, which is kept in front (not back) of his house. Almost like a status symbol. And it stinks like hell—not to mention its ugly, offensive appearance. If it smells badly now in the dead of winter, you can imagine the stench in the warm weather. I hope I'll be far away by then (meaning home). Chickens climb up the pile all day long, picking and pecking. Barns are part of the house and it's a familiar sight to see a barnyard animal living in the cellar—right below the kitchen and living room. We've spent many a night in their company! Along with the rest of the household.

Also, in front of the house is a big pump. Never a toilet inside. Existence is the only thing these villagers strive for. Beauty or convenience never enter the picture, and is of no consequence whatsoever.

Today, four of our Air Corpsmen "took to the silk" when they ran into plane trouble. Everything turned out OK and lots of the boys ripped up the parachutes for souvenirs. The "chute" is silk. I've been a little souvenir conscious lately, knowing we have a growing boy who'd get a thrill out of things from this part of the world. Picked up a few more coins and will enclose a couple each day.

The cooks are really spoiling us. Chicken again today (roast). With all my love.

26 January

Last night we received what we call PX rations and I'm involved with my "Special Service" problems this morning. The rations contain beer, cigars, candy for each boy and my job is to distribute the items and collect the money—about 25 francs each.

Again I enjoyed your account summary. Write about it often. Here, whenever something interesting happens during the day, someone says, "Another paragraph," meaning he'll have something new to talk about when he writes home. (We both know how hard it is at times to fill a letter.) Well, that will give you another paragraph. Me, too!

Right now we're listening to Berlin Sally on the radio—the girl who plays American records and tears up the Allies as German propaganda. We all get a kick out of it.

We got Sunkist oranges today—and delicious, too. A little change and much appreciated. They do try hard to give us the best.

You wonder why my cold lingers. You must realize, Honey, that although we live under cover a good deal of the time, the doors are open constantly, with boys coming in and out of the Station all day. Many times I rush out on errands—or a quick move in a freezing jeep, etc. But it was never anything serious—just a hanging-on cold. You know, living conditions here aren't even a reasonable facsimile of home!

4 February

Today I'm away from my group taking a 2-day "rest." Doc is rotating all of us back to rest camps, not only to clean up and see a couple of shows, but to get away from those damn weird mortars the boys call "screaming meemies." They sure can shake you up when they go shooting by.

Since noon I've eaten a hearty luncheon, sat in on a

musical jam session, saw a movie, took a bath and changed clothes, and then treated to a "risque" stage show put on by GIs. They go all out to make you comfortable here, and with the friendly, quiet atmosphere—what do you think it's doing to your husband? You're right, I'm homesick.

Over here, no one wears stripes or bars, except the privates. We call them "shower promotions." You see, when we take showers, we throw all our dirty clothes in, and pick up fresh ones. Quite often some private picks up a clean shirt formerly worn by a Sgt.—stripes and all—and in fun we call him a Sgt. When someone congratulates him on the promotion, he tells them he received a "shower promotion."

You asked me to describe the exact function of the Aid Station. First let me tell you how evacuation works: A boy gets hurt on the line. Within a minute or less a telephone message is sent back to our forward Aid Station, a distance of 300 to 1000 yds. from the front where a Sgt. and four litter bearers are always on hand. They rush right to the line with a litter.

During this time, the Company in which the casualty is a member has their Aid-man administering first aid on the spot—usually consisting of stopping the bleeding with Sulfanilamide powder externally, bandaging, and giving wound pills internally. By that time, another litter team is there and carries the casualty to the nearest point where a jeep can travel—anywhere from 25 to 3,000 yards, depending on conditions. The injured boy is then rushed to the Aid Station, one to three miles behind the line. Here the physician removes the first-aid bandage, makes a proper diagnosis and applies a more permanent bandage, administers blood plasma if needed, and in severe cases, gives morphine; makes the patient comfortable, warm, gives coffee, etc. Whereupon he's rushed back to a point known as Clearing Company pretty far in the rear—this time by a comfortable ambulance which

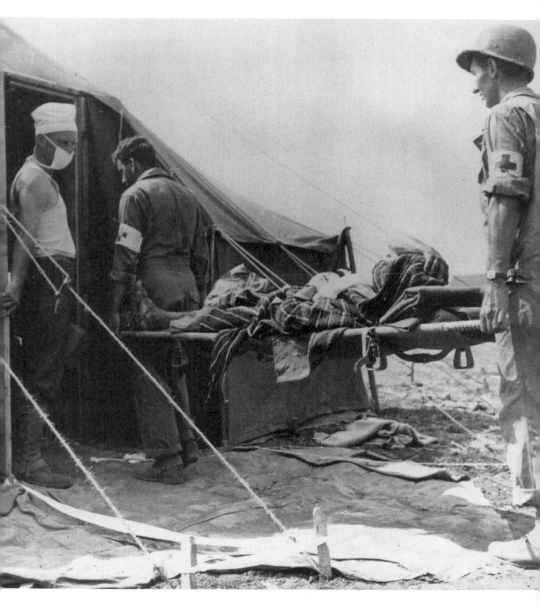

Soldiers wounded in battle were taken to aid stations behind the front line for treatment and were later evacuated to hospitals far to the rear.

stands ready for action at the Aid Station's door. Now here, if the wound requires it, he's given an emergency operation or attention. This place is well-staffed and well-equipped. Then the casualty is taken by ambulance to an Evacuation hospital further back where first-class attention is administered.

If the case is one whereby the wound or casualty is so severe and he won't get better very soon, he's shipped back even further to a General Hospital, and eventually back to the States.

Reason for the continual moves? One of room. As the patient warrants a further move back, he leaves space for another boy, and needed room is of the essence.

The Aid Station has no beds. Its job is the most important—to evacuate the wounded boy from place of incident to the rear, after essential treatment is administered to save his life. The well-equipped rear stations get the soldier and handle him with the skill that is possible only in a quiet hospital.

So you see, the Aid Station is equipped only with essentials. As each boy comes in (sometimes a half-dozen at once) I help with necessary details—proper bandages, blood plasma, fill out tag giving a brief history of the boy and his diagnosis, and what has been done for him. As each echelon does something more, it's added to the card, which is then tied to the buttonhole in the boy's coat, so that pertinent information stays right with him. This, then is the procedure with a front-line casualty.

Much of our work, too, has to do with ailments such as colds, flu, foot trouble, trench foot, etc. We treat them and they usually return to the line.

Am still hoping for an abrupt end before the month is out. It's funny—if funny is the word—how both of us live from month to month hoping for an end to it all. I believe we do this to keep ourselves going, for eventually, end it must. It appears however you'll have to plant the garden, though I may get to cultivate it—and surely eat it. O.K.? I always seem to miss out on the asparagus, though.

> The garden that Winston is referring to was called a Victory Garden. Growing Victory Gardens was an important civilian effort in which city and town people planted vegetables in small plots and in backyards. These gardens supplied civilians with vegetables they couldn't get in grocery stores. They were so successful that they actually produced one-third of all the vegetables grown in the United States during the war years. Besides Victory Gardens, Americans conserved material to help the war effort in other ways. One of the biggest efforts was collecting scrap to help make up for the shortage of raw supplies. Children were active "recyclers" as they collected cooking fat, newspapers, old sneakers (for their rubber content), and anything metal. The collected material was turned over to the Army and the Navy, to be used in an amazing variety of ways. Guns and tanks were 50 percent scrap metal, so were subs and ships. Scrap rubber was used to make gas masks, in fact one old tire provided eight gas masks. An old iron could be used to produce two helmets, 7,700 pans supplied aluminum for a pursuit plane, one refrigerator yielded three machine guns, 32 toothpaste tubes provided the tin for one plane, and 100 pounds of scrap paper made a carton for 35 shells.

15 February

No mail today, but a delicious package with everything I like in it, including the Sears catalog [the then-famous shop-by-mail catalog of Sears Roebuck and Company]—all of which was welcome.

The news of the 1,500-plane raid over Tokyo was indeed encouraging. Remember, the European conflict is only part of the war, and Tokyo is a big obstacle.

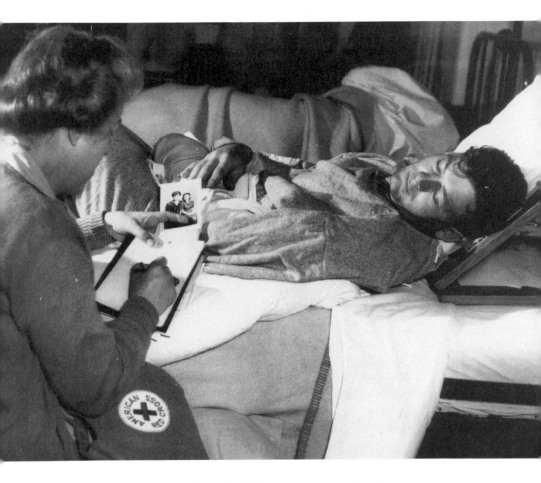

*In hospitals Red Cross workers helped
wounded soldiers with their letters home.*

Again we heard German propaganda in English,
knocking hell out of the Allies. You'd get a kick out of listening. It shows the real character of the German mind.
On the one side of their mouth they're reviling the terrible American and British raids on the poor refugees
leaving Berlin with "all their earthly belongings"—and

on the other side they're boasting how thorough their robots have been in devastating London. Just this minute I heard 2,000 bombers are over Berlin. It can't be long now.

We hear the boys are making fine progress over Japan. It sure makes me happy as it seemed that side of the war was being treated like a stepchild. The more extended that part becomes, the longer we'll be in the Army.

Darling, tonight as I sit here, many boys have stumbled in from the front line for some medical aid—"minor" reasons: stomach upsets, colds, foot trouble, etc. They're muddy and dirty and aching all over, and pathetically happy to be in under "real" light, where it's warm and comfortable, and away from where talking above a whisper could mean enemy rifleshot or a mortar sent screaming in their direction. They come at night; they can't get out of foxholes during the day for fear of being spotted. It tears me up to see them trudge back—and they do, even in pain because there are no replacements and the line has to be held. They know a buddy is depending on them.

Not only do they experience the horror of battle and noise—but also something just as deadly—and that's monotony, which is something terrible when you're holing up all the time.

Maybe I've told you this before, but these are the boys our country should be grateful for. They're nothing short of heroes.

6 March [Cablegram from Paris]
MY DARLING I AM HAVING A HOLIDAY IN A WONDERFUL CITY BUT MISSING YOUR COMPANIONSHIP MORE THAN YOU CAN EVER KNOW. ALL MY HEART.

6

PURSUING THE NAZIS

MARCH TO MAY 1945

On March 7, 1945, units of the American First Army were able to cross the Rhine River on the Remagen bridge and swarm into Germany. The Allies had originally planned for Field Marshal Montgomery's British forces to make the first crossing of the river, but once the Americans were able to get across they continued rolling through Germany as fast as possible. Keith Winston's 100th Division was in position inside Germany by the third week in March.

22 March, France

Darling, we're rolling now—really rolling. Don't worry, as a few more days like this and my chances of getting home sooner will be greater.

LATER: This morning we saw scores of haggard Russians walking toward our rear—prisoners the Nazis had used as slaves and left behind when the Krauts retreated. Darling, when I saw their faces—their smiles of joy, their revived hope—and American food in their hands, it brought tears to my eyes for I knew I was seeing firsthand just what we're fighting for—the right to be free, to go unmolested, to have freedom from oppressive tyranny—something these poor souls hadn't known for years.

It was one of the most heart-rending scenes I've encountered, and I've seen plenty. Among this group were many women, aged beyond their years. To see their faces when they saw us is an indescribable experience. I saw many a "hardened" soldier with tears streaming from his eyes. A terrible world we're living in, isn't it.

What I've seen of the land here is beautiful but it's all dimmed by these bestial circumstances. If only these people had concentrated on their beautiful country instead of trying to destroy the world. But it all backfired like a boomerang and they've destroyed themselves in the attempt.

If we soldiers have anything to say about it—and we will—this is the last war Germany will start.

24 March

We're still rolling and with a few more bridgeheads over the Rhine, I can't see how the momentum can be stopped.

For the first time I saw what our Air Force can really do and I take back every mean word I've ever said about them. It was our first opportunity to see the effectiveness of the last 3 or 4 years of bombing. The Nazis withheld the news, but we saw enough.

In one section we saw miles of German vehicles, tanks and supply dumps, horses and wagons virtually end to end—and everything completely demolished. Despite what is heard from German sources, make no mistake about it, they're suffering and suffering acutely. Their towns and cities have been shelled, even more so, bombed, and nothing is much worse than bombing. It undermines and shatters morale, not to mention the

The advancing American forces freed Russian soldiers held in German prison camps. Here Russian soldiers run cheering toward their American liberators.

country and materials. And they're showing it in more ways than one. Through the towns we've gone through, white flags of surrender hang from every window.

One of our German-speaking boys constantly hears the people bemoaning their state. They know the war is lost and they ask each other, "Why doesn't Hitler quit?"

25 March

Is it possible that one year ago today I left home for the Army? This year, with its heartaches and pain, has made a big change in our lives and when we're together again we'll appreciate life even more. Over here you see how precarious it can be from day to day. And you learn to take nothing for granted.

War is such a peculiar phenomenon. As I write this letter I can hear the city—close by—being bombed. I can see our planes overhead on their way to this city. And I can see the enemy flak pouring on them, trying to down our planes. If I watch closely, I can see the smoke rising as our planes lay their "eggs." Yet here we are just a short distance away, relaxing, waiting for the Air Force to soften this city so our force can go in and take it. God, war is weird.

In a letter you wrote a few weeks ago, you told me to have my gas mask with me at all times. Your wording was exactly the way our Colonel ordered it—and everyone got a kick out of the similarity of your "order." We realize that gas could be used any minute and always have our gas masks with us, Dear. However, I doubt if they'll resort to it as their own people will suffer, since the war now is right smack in the big German cities, heavily populated.

27 March

The thought of the folks back home making big plans for V-E [Victory in Europe] Day provoked me, when boys over here are still giving their blood, and plenty of it. Even though the reports already have the war won, remember, until V-E Day we're sweating out enemy artillery fire that goes with war. [Censored sentence.] Until the final second of victory, the boys are in there. Until then, there's no reason for celebration.

30 March

Still awaiting orders and expect a change soon. The word continues good, and again I repeat any hour could bring real news.

96

We listen to the German reports over the radio and since Mox talks German we enjoy getting their version—which is a continuation of fantastic lies. ["Mox" was the nickname of Max Haas, a member of Keith's company. Mox was a German Jew who had fled Hitler's Germany shortly before the start of the war. His family remained behind. The men dubbed him "Moxie," a slang term for nerve or courage, which was then shortened to Mox.]

Sometimes the American propaganda station broadcasts to the Germans in their language and gives the true picture. This morning he was talking in perfect German, when all of a sudden he says in English, "Excuse me,"—then "oh, my"—then continued quickly, "On shultish" (excuse me). He got his languages mixed and we all had a good laugh.

There was a picture story in "This Week" about a GI returning with a mangled hand—and about his adjustment. There will be thousands, perhaps hundreds of thousands, going through the same experience—probably worse.

1 April

We've left our old location and are presently comfortably quartered in a small bungalow, but will be moving again today.

Again I saw what our Air Force has been doing these last few years. Dear, you read and hear of so much devastation in Germany now—but I have seen big cities, very big cities—whose main areas are reduced to a pile of rubble, all bricks and stones. It's like a dream looking at all this especially when you see so many things directly connected to Hitler—huge swastikas on the remains of an airport and big buildings. It's hard to believe the things you read about are actual—but they are actual.

These towns we enter are newly Nazi-army freed villages, although the civilians, I assure you, are still Germans, and our orders are very strict—to be always

A U.S. Army evacuation hospital, seen from the air,
with Red Cross markings to signal German bombers
that the site was not a military target.

on guard, never to walk alone, and the stress is on fine or imprisonment if we fraternize. [The U.S. Army forbade soldiers to associate in a friendly way with the people of Germany.] The boys are holding fast to these rulings— and the Germans, knowing we enter as conquerors—not liberators as was the case in France—look on us with hate and loathing.

2 April

We visited an old city—close by—famous for its university and romanticized by Sigmund Romberg's beautiful music—and also for its castle which is world-renowned. It's truly one of the lovelier cities, and I enjoyed roaming around the streets. If this gets by the censors I'm sure you'll recognize the city.

4 April

On the "go" again. "On the go" means we'll be together again that much sooner. We're situated in a little village but ready to go again at any moment.

Why in hell doesn't someone come forth who could accept a peace? We now know that madman Hitler doesn't dare tell the Nazis to lay down their arms. He'd sooner see the country leveled, and he cares even less for the populace. Right now the only thing that matters is his own hide, which isn't worth a plugged nickel. And no one knows it better than he. But in the meantime our own boys suffer needlessly.

8 April

What better way of being greeted on a dismal morning than with a bright, 4-page letter from my sweetest one. It certainly did start the day off right. As you see by the above date, I missed a couple of days writing so you must know things have been hopping.

Yes, our Division does have a newspaper but the latest ruling is that we're not permitted to send it back home. It's called the Century Sentinel, is pretty good and comes out twice a month.

An appalling sight throughout the villages we travel is to see so many men and women with "P" or "R" on a patch sewn to their clothes. They're Poles or Russians who work as slaves for the German people—another example of their bestiality. Each community, according to size or political advantage, has an allotment of these "slaves." One village—say, about the size of Westgate— would be allotted 100 and disposed of at the discretion of the Burgermeister (mayor). Some of these people, we hear, have "found a home" and seem reasonably contented in these small towns where they have food to eat and a place to put their heads at night.

Others are migrating in tremendous numbers to the rear where they're placed in camps for eventual disposition to their homeland.

German civilians, in direct contrast to the French we've seen, are very healthy, proving they've been eating well and living under conditions comparable to Americans. They've been stealing food and labor and about everything else from their conquered nations. Here, everyone has electrical appliances—radios, irons, stoves, sewing machines, even electric razors. You see, they haven't been "deprived."

Something occurred today that brought the war even closer, and made me realize even more why Americans have no right to be softhearted or to forget that because of these Nazis many American boys are dead or maimed for life: A wounded Nazi was brought in (as many are during the day) and given aid—the best possible—and I don't begrudge that. But just as we'd finished dressing his wounds two wounded GIs walked in—and both, as they met the Nazi's eyes, said, "That's the bastard."

And then they spilled the story. This same Nazi kept sniping at their whole platoon as they went by, wounding them and three others. And as they waited for treatment—imagine, they had to wait (not many minutes, though) until the Jerry was finished being treated. And the incredible part: one Medic who spoke German questioned him in such a friendly way, "Are you married? Any children? Where do you live? How old?" etc. etc. Well, I burned to see this pleasant discourse carried on while our own GIs waited for attention—and waiting until the rat who shot them was treated first.

Could you imagine this being reversed? Well, I blew up and told this Medic and all the others that their function is not that of a welcoming committee and in the future they will refrain from uttering a word to the enemy. All questioning can and will be done by the interrogators. I assure you this Medic, or any other, will still treat the wounded enemy well—but that's where it will end.

9 April

A few days ago I viewed one of the most graphic and exciting sights I've ever seen. From an observation post I witnessed a battle. I could see our doughboys creeping and crawling and lying low—and off in the distance I could see the Nazis firing and rushing for cover when our mortars went off. Then I could see one of our Companies trying to outflank the Jerries—and then one of our men fall as he was hit. In very short order our litter-bearers were out there picking him up. At this point the battle was getting hotter and it was necessary for me to come down and get over to the Aid Station to attend the casualties. If only I had a moving picture camera! Rarely can you see a battlefield, showing the enemy at the same time. A war photographer would have had a real scoop. To allay your concern, I assure you I was up there a very short time—and would not go up again.

11 April

Another day, another move, another house, another village. These towns are picturesque—always on the side of a little river or stream, often with hilly terrain or mountains looming in the background. These "innocent" little rivers invariably present a big obstacle. As the Nazis are pushed back they blow up the bridge behind them, leaving us with a problem of crossing.

You can see that with problems like these a Battalion Aide Man is deeply concerned with evacuation—how to carry a man who's been hit back to the next rear echelon. Being Americans, with typical American ingenuity we've solved it. We string a cable across the river and evacuate by rowboat, using the cable as a guide. Always waiting on the other side is an ambulance with two drivers and four litter bearers. So far the evacuation has worked beautifully and we're proud of our record.

Winston does not mention to his wife that he and the other medics were under heavy fire from German artillery while the wounded were being evacuated by rowboat. The shelling was so intense that the 100th Division headquarters asked the 163rd Chemical Smoke Generator Company to lay a smoke screen over the river crossing to hide them. The 163rd was a black military unit. African Americans were restricted in job assignments and kept in segregated units during World War II. Two and a half million blacks registered for the draft, with most men serving in the army. However, black men and women served in all branches of the armed forces, except the Marines, which did not admit black women. Segregation in the American armed forces was ended in 1948.

13 April

The day was one of intense interest. Doc and I visited the German civilian hospital here and were surprised to find no doctor, little or no medicine, and only five nurses doing everything. Doc asked to be shown the worst cases and as we went through the halls, everyone glared at

African Americans served in segregated military units; here, a black artillery unit in action.

us—probably fearing an order to be moved out. We then entered a private room occupied by a mother and child, both of whom had been hit by shrapnel. The mother screamed bloody murder as the bandages were removed for Doc's observation. An infection had set in and Doc ordered an operation. So both she and her daughter are to be removed to a GI hospital.

While this was going on, an elderly woman came over to me, and in perfect English asked a number of questions. (She came in each day to help the nurses.) She said, "This country was so beautiful, and then he [Hitler] came to power and half the people were never for him. They [the Nazis] are beasts, I tell you beasts!" Her eyes filled with tears and she walked down the hall a few feet, turned around and cried out hysterically, "Beasts, Beasts!"

With the exception of a few nights when artillery was heavy I sleep soundly and look forward to bed and rest each night. Except for my homesickness, I am well and doing fine. How are Neil and David? Much of my day is in constant thought of them and you.

14 April

Last night, dead tired, we reached our destination at 2 A.M., only to hear that one of our boys was wounded. Since I was on the first vehicle I was called on to bring him back—and no time to spare. I led a group out—well over a mile—and we carried the boy all the way back. He weighed over 200 pounds and he seemed to get heavier with each step. Finally got in bed at 5 A.M. and awakened at 8:30 for another move. So-o-o I'm pretty bushed as I write you this lunch time.

I've just come up from a dark, damp cellar where we treated a German soldier who deserted a week ago when wounded. There were a dozen mattresses on the floor where people lay in fear of our bombers and artillery—and in terror of our soldiers.

My Darling, this minute I have just learned of our President's death. I am shocked and dazed at the terrible news. May God bless his soul. He was our friend. The world will suffer.

104

President Franklin Delano Roosevelt died in Warm Springs, Georgia, on April 12, 1945. V-E Day arrived just a few days short of a month later.

16 April

The war is supposed to be over, but these fanatics we're meeting don't know anything about it. It just adds up to more soldiers wounded and killed—including our own. Destruction is everywhere. A large city we recently took was unqualifiedly—except for a hospital—just a series of piles of stone and rubble. Even here our boys had to fight from shamble to shamble to clear the city. Small "pockets" (back home they speak of these as inconsequential—nothing) often keep a Regiment busy for days—with many deaths resulting.

Darling, I'm getting accounts of the President's death—its significance, the reactions of the men all around. We feel that we've personally suffered a loss. I can't tell you how much all this has saddened us.

Patton and the British 9th have made fine infiltrations and things look very good. Haven't heard much from the Pacific theater, but hope for a more sensible attitude from the Japs when all doubt of our victory here is removed.

26 April

We're located in still another house. Doc just returned from Paris, seems rested and in a better frame of mind.

Our Aid Station is located in a large apartment house. Every couple of guys has a two-room apartment, but have to share their bathroom and kitchen with two other guys—mighty inconvenient, isn't it! Doc and I share the same apartment. We all have radios, and beds with clean linen. There might be a good chance we'll be here awhile, and we're looking forward to clean clothes and hot baths.

The radio tells us Bremen is taken, Berlin almost

*President Franklin Roosevelt, delivering a radio
address about six months before his death*

taken, and the Italian patriots taken over in northern Italy. All looks "encouraging." And now we hear Goebbels resigned—and Mussolini is running out. Sounds good, Sweetheart.

> Benito Mussolini, Italy's dictator, and his mistress were captured on April 26, 1945 by Italian partisans and were executed two days later. Joseph Goebbels, Hitler's propaganda minister, poisoned his six children and had himself and his wife shot the day after Hitler killed himself on April 30.

Today's movements took me again through this beautiful land. I usually ride in the ambulance but Doc asked me to ride with him in the jeep. (Vision isn't too good in the ambulance.) The scenery is indescribably breathtaking—but I'd trade it all for South Street if it meant being with you.

Remember Mox? (Max Haas) the Jewish refugee boy who had relatives over here? Today we heard a rending, pitiful story. He was finally able to visit his hometown, and when he got to his old house, the occupants told him his parents had been sent to Lublin concentration camp 3 years ago—and you know what that means—wholesale slaughter. The poor guy. You should have seen him when he came back. His eyes were red and swollen, his face wet with tears. No one or nothing could console him.

The boys were tripping over one another trying to make him feel a little better. What can you say to a boy with a tragedy so decimating as his. No one could find the right words. Even Chuck, the "rough" GI from Arkansas, who's never at a loss for words. Then he stuttered, his voice husky with emotion, "God damn, Mox, I'll git me a rifle and go out pussonly and pick off a few Krauts. Them lousy, heartless sonofabitches." He was dead serious, and even Mox smiled through his tears.

*As the Allies freed the German-held territories
and entered the concentration camps, the full
horror of the Nazi atrocities came to light.*

28 April

Today has been one of restfulness. We saw a movie,
Judy Garland in Meet Me in St. Louis, and it was beautiful.
Not the story so much, which I couldn't follow as I
arrived half an hour late and the Vitaphone [movie

soundtrack] was lousy—but just to see an American setting, with American songs and Americans was a real treat.

Himmler, the radio tells us, offered his historic acceptance of unconditional surrender—but only to us and the English. It did my heart good to know we'd do nothing without Russia. Unquestionably, we are and should be a trio never to be divided. I assure you the boys on the front line will always fight for this combination—particularly U.S. and Russia. Oh, boy, do the Germans fear them. You can't begin to imagine the hatred and fear the little German—the average German—has of the Russian. Why? First, the Russians wiped out hordes of them. 2nd, the Germans having used Russians as slaves, now fear reprisals. 3rd, though German propaganda has been going all out to cover up the atrocities perpetrated upon thousands and thousands of poor, innocent Russian civilians, everyone knows their attempts at whitewashing are a lot of claptrap and won't do the Nazis one little bit of good.

The boys are getting closer to Munich, the Bavarian capital, where peace riots are reported. Any day, Darling.

29 April

It's Sunday night but I'm not listening to Walter Winchell or Phil Baker or Fred Allen [popular American radio personalities] as we did together. I'm just contenting myself with thoughts of you, and looking forward to the day when we'll always be together again. With all the good news coming in, how can it last many more days?

Just heard great news. Our troops have taken Munich and released 25,000 American prisoners! How about that! 25,000 boys and their loved ones are reborn tonight. Three of these poor fellows had supper with us. They talked very little because they were gulping food like animals. It broke your heart to watch them. May God help us end this murder soon.

109

1 May

Just heard Hitler is dead. So what. Even if he's alive, he's dead now. I'm only interested in hearing one thing—"The war is over!"

4 May

Feeling well, living comfortably—with little or no artillery racket, ours or theirs. The war here is just about over—certainly is in Germany, and finished up in Czech. and a few "pockets" in Austria. Just heard of Holland, Denmark's surrender—and now await Norway's, at which time Eisenhower will make his long-awaited announcement.

VICTORY
IN EUROPE
MAY TO AUGUST 1945

7 May 1945

TODAY IS THE DAY WE'VE WAITED AND SWEATED FOR.

Yes, I'm very happy, but somehow I can't get too excited about it. Why? I'm still here—and you're still there—and miles and months between us.

Yes, Honey, the war is over but the joy diminishes when I think of all the boys who've lost their lives in the struggle and are not here to enjoy the victory always uppermost in their minds. And all the boys in terrible shape languishing in hospitals. Some of them better off dead. Basket cases. Physically and mentally.

And my sadness knowing that our President, instrumental in our victory, is not here to enjoy the results of his efforts—and not here to guide us on to complete victory, and hopefully, a lasting peace.

I know my spirits should be higher since we do have more to look forward to now, Darling. But I know you'd understand if you had seen all I have seen.

*All London turned out to celebrate V-E Day,
along with jubilant American servicemen.*

Here's the latest demobilization plan—can be
changed hourly. First, 300,000 men to be discharged
according to points. Figure me out under that plan what
with boys who've served 3, 4 or 5 years—with 1 to 3
years overseas duty. However, there's still a glimmer of

112

hope. Of the 700,000 men to be discharged by age and dependents, I may stand a slim chance. But let's not expect too much—and hope and pray for an early reunion—and above all that I'm not shipped out of the States once I'm returned.

In a day or two we're due for our battle star. Many of the boys feel we were gypped as our outfit is given only one star for the battle of Germany, and we actually participated in the liberation of France. But I can assure you I'm far from worried about it. You know my feelings about stars. And one star I don't want—a So. Pacific star!

We're now located in the Western entrance of the Bavarian mountains, 60 or 70 miles from Munich. I'd be happy if we stayed right here until we're to be shipped home.

Keith Winston refers to the May 7, 1945 unconditional surrender of the German High Command. The documents were actually signed on May 8 and this date marks the end of World War II in Europe. In the following months, delegates from fifty nations signed the United Nations Charter in San Francisco, the Potsdam Conference took place, and the Allies divided Germany into four military occupation zones. Winston mentions, as he has in previous letters, his sorrow over President Roosevelt's death before the end of the war. However, he doesn't say much about the new president, Harry S. Truman. Within a very short period, President Truman would have to decide whether to drop atom bombs to hasten the end of the war with Japan.

9 May

We had a parade today—not necessarily a victory parade, but a "dry run" practice in preparation for a Division parade next week. Six months of active combat

*En route to the Potsdam Conference, aboard
an American ship, President Harry Truman
enjoyed mess with crew members.*

didn't seem to take away any of the first-class soldiering our Division is famous for. They're OK.

I've heard many reports, maybe rumors, on the demobilization plan and still hang on to the hope I'll be home before the summer is out. However, everything depends on the progress of the Jap war.

114

The final defeat of Germany didn't seem to make a whole lot of difference here. The boys have no way of celebrating, no place to go and they're still in the same war set-up—no closer to home, and perhaps missing it a little more, especially in view of the jubilation, the celebrations back home, and knowing they're not a part of it.

As for the civilians, they considered the war over when we took over this town. The only difference is that they don't have to run to their "bungas" (air shelters) and no more fear for their lives, or that their homes would be "kapoot" anymore.

Well, Dearest, tomorrow we move again—probably to a little more permanent a setting than this one.

11 May

We try to keep busy with sports, hikes, jeep rides, but they don't satisfy. And educational programs, which have been promised, are not due for 60 days.

Last night we filled out our "deployment" sheets which figured credit on the basis of (1) Service in the Army, (2) Overseas credit, (3) Battle decorations, (4) Dependents. Unfortunately I'm way below par on length of service and overseas credit and the only group where I stand a chance is Age and Dependency. As to decorations, I have the Purple Heart, German Campaign Star, and a Bronze Star pending.

With little to keep them occupied at this point in the war, the soldiers were absorbed in figuring out the point system. The number of points determined when a soldier got to go home and was the topic of almost every conversation. Daily, they checked into new reports or rumors of how many points they could get for various service records, time in the army and medals. Much of Keith's correspondence is devoted to counting up his points to see when he might be sent home. This great push to bring the troops home was one reason why Truman was later criticized for not keeping a large enough force in Europe as part of the Army of Occupation.

17 May

Now I'm able to tell you that we're located close to Stuttgart. Was in this same area on that "rest" when the war ended. I can tell you, too, it was our Division that was put in the 7th Army Reserve as the war was coming to an end. Reserve actually means "held" for emergency if the call arises—fortunately, it didn't. Our outfit, I may have told you, was on the front line for over 170 straight days, and that is a record for the 7th Army.

Speaking of whether or not my job is considered combat—you can bet your stars it is. Now that danger is over I can speak freely and tell you I consider myself a very lucky guy in not getting killed or hit. Rarely did a day pass that it couldn't have happened.

Our Medical Section of 32 men was by far the luckiest in the Division—even with that we lost two (killed) and at least six seriously injured, missing death by a hair. At least 10 more were injured to the extent of being evacuated to England. The two dead boys were good friends of mine, so you can imagine how I feel. One, in particular, Ellis, must have had a premonition something might happen as he gave me his brother's address two weeks before he was killed. He asked me to write him of the details should anything happen. I was pretty shaken up about it. I plan to write when I get home. I can't seem to get myself to do it now.

As far as combat is concerned, Darling, unfortunately it means practically nothing—a battle star meaning only 5 points. It's appalling in view of the fact that a combat man risks his life every second of 24 hours. I have spo-

Medics worked in all areas of the war zone, on the front line and to the rear. Here, by way of an armored vehicle serving as an ambulance, medics reached a wounded soldier alongside a road.

ken to these men, and ten minutes later carried them into the Aid Station on a litter as casualties. And almost six straight months of it. One's hair can and does turn gray.

Of course, all Medics are not combat men. However,

if you're in the Infantry and attached to one of the Battalions, you're actually on the front line—no ifs, ands or buts. All battalions are made up of 32 Medics, and it's up to the Bn. Surgeon (Doc, in our case) to use these men to the best advantage. Eleven are Aid-men—the roughest and least glorified job in the Army. Ask any Infantryman and he'll tell you. He speaks of his Medic with reverence. Then there are 12 litter bearers, of which I was one when fighting was toughest. When a guy got hit on the front line we went out and got him. We picked up a boy one day in German territory while our own Infantrymen kept shooting over our heads to keep the enemy down. That's just one instance.

Yet for all the danger and risk to our lives—5 points are added to our score. Any guy on the front should receive no less than 5 points per month of combat credit. People back home don't have the slightest conception what combat means—not the slightest. They may think they know, but until they've been running for cover with airplanes strafing them, with 88s screaming over their heads—they just don't know. There are so many instances I can tell you about—things that make me shudder as I think of them.

22 May

In your letter today you ask about the current situation on points. As of now the frozen figure is 55. When I get my Bronze Star it will be good for 5 more. How quick medals take on importance! I agree with you that the whole thing is a farce. I think it would be fair to institute two categories. One on the point basis, and another on the age-dependency basis, dismissing a smaller but substantial number.

Another thing—these lousy combat ribbons should not count. The Air Medal is handed out like a prize in a Cracker Jack box while the Infantryman gets no such

118

opportunity. Remember, 9 out of 10 heroes never get a medal—and why should a Purple Heart count 5 points when another guy who's had shells fall around him, but never got hit, receive less credit. He may not be struck physically by a bullet but his mental state is stricken, often for life. In the Army they have to see blood before you're considered a "hero."

24 May

Today was lucky for your husband. He got four letters that raised his morale beaucoup de points.

Heinrich Himmler committed suicide. Other good news? I got 5 more points today. Our Division was awarded another battle star for our drive toward the Rhine. So now I have 60 points. Stuttgart is a large city—about 300,000 people in normal times. Now it's literally flat.

Heard over the radio that the whole First Army is on their way home already. If there are facilities for a full army of 75,000 to 100,000 all at once, shipping is not as bad as we're led to believe.

Heinrich Himmler was the chief of the Gestapo in Nazi Germany from 1936 to 1945. Next to Hitler, he was the most powerful man in Germany. Although he was with Hitler from the very beginning of the dictator's rise to power, Himmler left Hitler to die in a bomb shelter in Berlin, and tried to seek safety for himself by negotiating secretly with the United States or Britain. His one-man peace mission failed and he was captured by the British on May 21, 1945, near the city of Bremen. On May 23, he swallowed poison and died shortly afterward.

7 June, Waiblingen

Now we're in Waiblingen, a beautiful city not far from Schorndorf, where I was stationed when the war ended.

In about two weeks we'll move on to Schorndorf to receive some SOP (Standard Operational Procedure) training—stuff only needed in garrison life, not to win wars. All this damn theory is only given in garrison, but in real combat little or none is used. It really nauseates and this is no exaggeration.

16 June

Am getting so sick of all this, especially after hearing that 86% of the U.S. people (who know nothing—zero—of the hell a soldier endures) want unconditional surrender with Japan. It's so easy to want all—when you give nothing.

We're about finished with the typhus shots and that's a relief. How is David? I hope no German measles. German, no less!

24 June

Today is Sunday, and again you came through. I love you, Darling for never letting me down.

Everything points to our heading toward the States soon. Our Division is now in Class 2B—meaning we're slated for the Pacific by way of the U.S. I'm certain Occupation is out.

Being in the Army is so difficult for men like me. Some of these kids have found "a home" in the Army, but I find it harder and harder to take being away from my family. If the Pacific struggle would end abruptly everything would work out. Darling, we're just going to find some way to make up for all this lost time.

29 June

My Bronze Star was finally awarded officially—by written order—and I know you'll be pleased. I'm pleased, too. It means 5 more points! And points are mighty precious these days.

120

4 July

Your letter came in and few letters could have been better timed on this extra-lonely "holiday."

We hear by the radio the Japs are talking peace. Nothing official, but after what our bombers have done in a short time they must realize what another bombing can do to a city, and a people's morale. You can't conceive what it means till you yourself are on the receiving end. It's the most fearful, terrifying, ghastly feeling—especially when you hear children wailing.

Again rumor. This time our Battalion is up for the Presidential citation. It's a unity award the boys are pulling for since there's quite an honor attached to it. We'd be given a blue ribbon to be worn on the right breast (other ribbons on the left)—but with all that "honor," no points are attached to it. We also hear the French are presenting the Division with the highest French unit citation—the croix de guerre—for our successful attack on Bitche—the first time in history this tremendous fortress was taken by force. I still feel the same about ribbons, but I'd wear every one of them if they'd mean points to get me home! They're good souvenirs, anyway.

6 July

Darling, it's very hard for me to write the following, but the facts must be faced. Our General (Burress) just returned from the States and advises that we'll probably not move until March. We're considered "Strategical Reserve" as you know, and we're here for anything (uprising, etc.) that might arise. He further stated we're not headed for the States until all 85 pointers and wounded, etc. and priority Divisions are shipped. Of course orders, plans and the like can be changed as conditions change in the Pacific, but I'll have to admit I'm very much upset about it, Darling. I feel the Jap war is coming to an end and I'd hate to be caught over here when it does.

When Japan attacked Pearl Harbor on December 7, 1941, Americans reacted with rage against the Japanese nation and often referred to its people as "Japs" or used other derogatory terms, as they had similarly vented anger at the Germans with such names as Krauts and Huns.

9 July

Today's Stars & Stripes announced our Division will not be leaving this year, reiterating the General's announcement. We were hoping against hope and it was a real sock between the eyes. Especially since the Army has done nothing about keeping the boys occupied. No organized instruction in anything; even passes to the big cities have been cut since cessation of hostilities. Oh, yes, just imagine—boys with over 2 years of college are permitted to study in the Sorbonne or Oxford—that is, if you're lucky to be one of the 800 chosen in the 7th Army—a ratio of 1 to a thousand. Big Deal.

15 July

Yesterday we traveled around until 10 P.M. and when I came "home" I found two of the dearest letters anyone could ask for.

Our day of travel was an eye-opener—interesting and frightening—something I wish everyone in the world could see, and then I don't believe there'd ever be another war. First, we saw Stuttgart again, and as you view it from the top of a mountain (Stuttgart lies in a tremendous valley) it looks like a picture of Greek ruins. As you look at it you think you're dreaming—this just can't be true. The contrasts are weird—beautiful countryside and indescribable devastation. We drove until we came to Pforzheim, a village the size of Upper Darby [near Philadelphia], demolished—leveled.

*As GIs moved into German towns, the full
extent of the war's devastation became evident.*

Then to Heidelberg—quaint, picturesque—untouched
by war (except for the bridges over the Neckar blown
up by the Nazis)—its beauty incomparable. Heidelberg is
nestled in a gigantic valley on either side of the Neckar

River. We kept driving along the Neckar, through portions of the Black Forest, breathtaking in itself, with its many mountains and dense forest as far as the eye can see.

Then finally to Beerfelden, the home of Mox. Even after all these years, everywhere Mox went crowds of people gathered, for they all remembered him well. It was tough for him to go back again to this town where they dragged his parents off, but for some reason of his own, he seemed to want to. We had quite a time earlier, but all this was such deep trauma for Mox we came away feeling lousy. He was silent all the way back, and no one said a word as we were all feeling his despair.

I'm relieved you're accepting the fact I'll be here awhile—and as long as I have to, I'll make the best of it—taking courses (if and when), trips, going out on "quartering" parties, or whatever else may present itself.

2 August

Today another rumor—nothing official—but the boy insists it's authentic—that we're to replace the 63rd Division on the return home timetable. According to him we're due home the first week in December. Hope it's true but won't believe it until I'm getting off the boat in New York harbor.

Sam [Samuel Cahoon, Staff Sergeant, later Lieutenant, also assigned to the Aid Station] just told me our outfit stands a good chance of getting a 3rd battle star—which will mean 70 points for me. A campaign star for the Vosges campaign is now being considered by the General. That was by far the worst part of our entire action. Sam was told this by a Lt. whose father is a Brig. General with the deployment of troops in the ETO [European Theater of Operations] and he's repeating what his father told him—that as things stand now we'll be on our way to a

European P.O.E. the latter part of October or early November, so-o-o let's cross our fingers and hope—but not plan.

Your enjoyment on receiving 5 more crates [souvenirs that Winston sent home for Sarah and the boys] seems to rub off on me. I had to smile at your reaction to the rickety U.S. mail truck stopping regularly at the house—and the driver's remark, "Another surprise from your soldier today." And your and Neil's excitement as you rush to pry open the cases, like "digging into a grab bag," not knowing exactly what you'll find—and your "squeals" of joy, your "tingling" feeling at the sight of a mail truck, associating it directly with me. You can't imagine how much pleasure this gives me.

7 August

What a world we live in. I guess you've heard about Hiroshima's bombing. God, how I hate to hear of innocent people being victims. There must never be another war as the next time the whole world could be destroyed. War is a literal hell, everyone suffers—it's a series of horrors.

That disposition rumor of leaving in late October is gaining weight, which means we'd be hitting the States in Dec. if true. Neil's prayers may be taking effect—since "he isn't saying that for his health." I got a kick out of that remark, and I'm pleased with his progress on the piano. With your violin, my clarinet, and David's pot-lids we could make a quartet!

In one of your letters you say, "I have a feeling in my heart that something will turn up that will bring us together sooner than we now dream." You might have had a psychic feeling that our shipping orders had been set earlier. Now I hear we leave Waiblingen about Sept. 1 and to the States October 1—the last is pure rumor. By the way, we expect to go to Rheims, and will (in the next 30-odd days) get to Paris once in awhile. Am being "paged" now, Honey.

In July 1945, while the Potsdam Conference was in session, the first atomic explosion was set off in New Mexico. The conference drafted an ultimatum calling on the Japanese to surrender. When President Truman did not receive a satisfactory answer from Tokyo, he authorized the Air Force to drop two atomic bombs on Japanese cities. The atom bombs were actually dropped on Hiroshima on August 6 and Nagasaki on August 9, 1945.

PEACE
AT LAST

AUGUST TO DECEMBER 1945

13 August

Well, Dearest, it looks good. We plan—officially—to leave between August 24th and 27th and go direct to Le Havre, and GET THIS—leave no later than Sept. 10. Yes, Sept. 10! So it's possible I may be home before Neil's birthday. Isn't that great news! Even with a Jap surrender I believe we'll go through with it—and it sure will be better sweating out a discharge in the States than in Europe—what say! Now, as far as mail, keep writing, but send no packages. It's pretty likely I'll be going to [Fort] Dix—the closest separation center to our home. It would be great for you to drive over—about a $3/4$-hour ride— meet me, and we can go back together. How does that sound? Of course, I'll call you and make all the arrangements—when, where, and if. Things sure do happen fast, don't they. For the next three days we'll be busy giving physicals to the Companies.

Even though it will be a boat trip—and I dread them

because of my susceptibility to "mal de mer"—I guess I'll be able to take it 'cause I'll be a-headin' home.

14 August

Well—the letters came—6 of them! I can see you're sweating it out just as I am.

Sweetheart, quit sitting on "pins and needles." You should know by this time the Army moves like molasses. The grand old Army motto: Hurry up—and wait. Relax and accept the fact that if the Division moves I'll be home before you know it.

Today I and several others were awarded the Bronze Star in person, by no less a dignitary than General Burress—our Division General—and a better one you couldn't want. We all like and respect him as he's 100% behind the boys, always. It was quite a ceremony—band and parade. Please hang on to the citation I sent you earlier.

It's supposed to be a "holiday" around here today, but really not any different than elsewhere. A few of the boys took a ride to Beerfelden to get Mox, who's been there two weeks on Detached Service. Ever since he learned about his parents' fate he's not been the same. He always had a good sense of humor, but now he rarely smiles, and when he does he looks pathetic. It's pretty sad. I hope he snaps out of it soon.

18 August

Had a good letter from you today and it did help—although I'll admit not too much. Why? Our Division

The scene below deck of a troop ship returning from Europe; and the scene on deck of a victory ship docking in New York Harbor.

heard that our trip to the States is postponed—one, two, or three months. It hurts me to tell you this as I know you're just about at your wit's end, taking all this alone. And now I'm actually no closer to home than I've been in the last eleven months—with very little immediate prospect. And, Sweetheart, please don't anticipate a thing until you hear me calling you up from a telephone in the States. You must remember that. Please try to relax a little. Let the house go, save your energy for the children, for that's the important thing. Oh, I know it's easy for me to talk, with you back home sweating out every hour of every day. But something must give over here, it can't go on indefinitely.

26 August

The radio just reported that the point system is now abolished—and that all troops other than occupational will be home by the end of the year. I hardly believe anything I hear anymore, but if this is true, that is good news.

Wednesday I'll be taking a trip to Switzerland and look forward to a complete change of scene. God, would I love these trips with you here.

One thing I look forward to especially, Darling, is calling you up on the phone from Switzerland. I can't wait to hear your voice.

Although Winston doesn't mention it, the papers that ended the war in the Pacific were signed on September 2, 1945, aboard the battleship *Missouri,* in Tokyo Bay. World War II was over.

6 September, Zurich, Switzerland

I'm still in Zurich and despite not hearing from you last night, cling to the hope your call may yet come in—though we leave this city at 3 P.M. and it's now 11 A.M.

This is the "heart" of Switzerland, and not unlike 5th

Avenue or Chestnut Street. It is busy, beautiful and has about everything. Since I last wrote I visited Lucerne on Lake Lucerne. Switzerland—its lakes, mountains, little villages, and large cities, is quaint, romantic and very modern in the midst of medieval architecture. Books or travel agencies can't adequately describe it.

We leave for Basel this afternoon, stay overnight, then back to Waiblingen. Darling, I want so much for your call to come through—I'll then know I'm getting the latest about you and the children. But time is moving, and still no call.

25 September

Another rumor—not official—we're scheduled to meet a boat leaving Le Havre on the 15th. In the meantime, address all your mail to the Medical Detachment 398th Infantry. In two days I'll know the address of my new outfit. I'll have to admit I'm pretty excited about everything.

Today, my last day with the Division and I've been running around getting things set before I leave. You know, it's a funny thing but I have ambivalent feelings about leaving. On the one hand I can't wait to get away, and count every minute—and yet it's going to be hard to leave so many friends who have been through so much with me. But when I realize my leaving means coming home to you, I can't feel badly at all. Along with me come a couple of friends from the Aid Station, and that helps a lot.

26 September, Gerstetten, Germany

Well, Darling, I am now a "tank-man"—12th Armored Division. Rumor has it we'll leave for the boat in 13 days, and for the States Oct. 15th. Not official—just rumor. We're on the last lap of our separation. We'll be together soon—perhaps this time next month. Not much to do

131

here and I'm planning to visit the old outfit Saturday. Our comfort is nil compared to Waiblingen, but I can stand it for the reason we're here.

Although I won't be getting your mail here for awhile, keep writing until I learn the exact situation. Well, Dearest, every day means one day closer to home.

3 October, Waiblingen

The latest has it that we Medics will receive combat pay, retroactive from January. So-o that will be welcome. Oh, yes, we're to be stationed at Camp Baltimore in Rheims (that's official). Rheims is about 50 to 80 miles from Paris I believe.

We must be on the right wavelength—your talking about the hotel and all was exactly what I had previously written you. Those snapshots of me make me out better than I am. I am tired and a little older looking, really.

So you're still receiving boxes! It makes me happy to hear of your consistent pleasure in their contents.

10 October, Gerstetten

As I write you, I'm sitting in an open field. It's a lovely clear, sunny day; and I can see miles and miles of open country. This land—away from the Division—is beautiful.

You know what I've been craving for? A thick slice of vanilla layer cake with vanilla icing and gobs of whipped cream. And milk, milk, milk, and more milk. We don't get fresh milk and we really need it. Our systems are not up to snuff and I think it might be a lack of calcium foods.

It's so pleasant here in the fields, the weather perfect—and I miss you terribly. Again I repeat, take things easy and don't do any redecorating or cleaning up for me as I won't appreciate it.

As long as we have a meeting of minds re: our vacation, I'll ask you to make the plans. However, first I want to be home a few days as I gotta see the kids and get to

132

Home at last

know them—not run out on them. You just don't know how I want to see those children.

1 November

My Darling, after all the Le Havre talk, it appears official that we'll be leaving around the 6th—and due to arrive in—listen to this—Marseilles—before the 12th. And last-minute processing to be completed by the 16th. And from there on we board the first ship available. The Stars & Stripes have us in the States before the end of the month which means exactly one month behind original plans.

This evening we've been discussing our needs in civilian clothes—it seems that we had all read the same article in this week's Yank about civilian clothing. I figured I'd have to spend about $150 to outfit myself. Does that sound about right?

My anxiety gets higher with each day closer to home, and my letters shorter, it seems. But I know you understand what pressure we're under, especially with nothing to do and nothing to say.

15 November, Marseilles

My Darling, here I am in Marseilles, where I landed exactly 13 months ago—but this time I'm a-comin' home—and soon. Thank God I'm actually on the way— we know how many times in these last months I've come close to missing it. But that's all over and done with— I'm really coming home!

As I write you now, I vividly recall sitting here in the same Red Cross Club writing you—a little over a year ago. What hell we've both been through since.

The reality of going home is clear now and his letters reflect that feeling. Keith Winston, and all other honorably discharged veterans who served between 1939 and 1946 received the honorable service lapel

134

To honor those who lost their lives in the Holocaust, and also those who survived, those who rose above the hatred to save Jews and other victims, and those who liberated the Nazi camps, the United States Holocaust Memorial Museum was dedicated in Washington, D.C., in April 1993.

pin. It was known by the nickname "Ruptured Duck." The origin of the nickname is not known, but the phrase had been painted on a B-25 bomber that was part of the "Doolittle Raid," a daring bombing attack on the Japanese homeland in April 1942, led by Colonel James H. Doolittle.

21 November

My Darling, Today will probably be the last day I spend on European soil. We expect to sail tomorrow—Thanksgiving Day—and will arrive in New York about December 4th. We'll head straight for Camp Shanks or Kilmer to be processed further, and outfitted with a complete set of new clothes. Whereupon I'll be sent to Indiantown Gap for discharge.

We are crossing on a Liberty ship and if it's anything like the trip over, I'm anticipating 10 days of seasickness, but with one major difference—it will be homeward bound this time. What can I say now except that I am terribly excited about happenings to come in the next two weeks. I must admit that I can hardly contain my exhilaration at the thought of our joyous reunion.

Until later, my Sweetheart. But this time—not by letter.

Your always loving husband
Keith

Pfc. Keith Winston landed in New York City in early December, 1945. He was discharged from the Army on December 10, 1945 and soon returned to his job with the insurance company. The company had held a place for him upon his return to civilian life. The United States was better prepared to help the men and women of the armed services re-enter civilian life at the end of World War II than after World War I. Jobs were plentiful because the American economy was still expanding. The GI Bill of Rights gave veterans who had been inducted during the war the opportunity for education and training for peacetime careers.

The United States emerged from this war with a heightened sense of global responsibility. When the fighting ended the United States quickly stepped in to help feed the starving people of Europe and to help rebuild their cities. America encouraged democracy and offered support to the fledgling democratic governments that emerged from the collapse of the Axis powers. The estimated war expenditures for the United States were $350 billion, and over a quarter of a million battle deaths. Worldwide, World War II costs totaled at least $4 trillion, and forty million dead civilians and military personnel.

FOR FURTHER
READING

Adler, David. *We Remember the Holocaust.* New York: Henry Holt, 1989.

Amdur, Richard. *Anne Frank.* New York: Chelsea House, 1993.

Devaney, John. *America Goes to War, 1941.* New York: Walker, 1991.

——. *America on the Attack, 1943.* New York: Walker, 1992.

Emmerich, Elsbeth, and Robert Hull. *My Childhood in Nazi Germany.* New York: Bookwright, 1992.

Hoobler, Dorothy, and Thomas Hoobler. *An Album of World War II.* New York: Franklin Watts, 1977.

Litoff, Judy B., and David C. Smith, eds. *Since You Went Away: World War II Letters from American Women on the Homefront.* New York: Oxford University Press, 1991.

McGowen, Tom. *World War II.* New York: Franklin Watts, 1993.

Marx, Trish. *Echoes of World War Two.* Los Angeles: Lerner Publications, 1993.

Scoggin, Margaret C., ed. *Battle Stations: True Stories of Men in War.* New York: Alfred A. Knopf, 1960.

Stevenson, James. *Don't You Know There's a War On?* New York: Greenwillow Books, 1992.

Vail, John J. *World War II: The War in Europe.* San Diego, Calif.: Lucent Books, 1991.

INDEX

Sgt. (sergeant), 21
"Shower promotions," 87
63rd Division, 124
Sleeping bag, 83
Special Orders, 34–35
Standard Operating Procedure (SOP), 120
Stars & Stripes, 62, 74, 122
Star-Spangled Banner, 51
Stockings, 20
"Strategical Reserve," 121
Stuttgart, 116, 122

Telephone hookups, 82
Tent, army, 69
Thanksgiving letter, 65–66
3rd Bn. Hq. Medical Section, 65
398 Infantry Regiment, 14, 45
Tokyo, raid on, 90
Tracer bullets, 37
Transition range, 40
Troopship, *128*
Truman, Harry S., 113, *114*, 116, 126
12th Armored Division, 131

United Nations Charter, 113
United States, costs of war of, 137; global responsibility of, 137
USO (United Service Organization), 42–43

V-E (Victory in Europe) Day, 96, *112*
Victory Garden, 89–90

Victory Ship, *128*
V-mail, 52, 53, *66*
Vosges campaign, 124
Vosges Mountains, 55, 72

Waiblingen, 119, 125, 132
Walensky, Alma Klein, *70*
Winchell, Walter, 31
Winston, David, 14, 47, *50*, 64, 120, 125
Winston, Keith, *13, 50, 84;* in basic training, 15–38; as civilian, 136; in combat, 56–77; at Ft. Bragg, 39–48, *40*; in Medical Corps, 48; meeting, 11–14; as PFC, 79; as tank man, 131; V-mail letter, *66*
Winston, Neil, 14, 25, 41, *50*, 64, 65–66, 125
Winston, Sarah, 14
Women, in armed forces, 61–62
Women Accepted for Volunteer Emergency Service (WAVES), 62
Women's Airforce Service Pilots (WASPs), 61
Women's Army Auxiliary Corps (WAAC), 61
Women's Auxiliary Ferrying Squadron (WAFS), 61
Women's Flying Training Detachment, 61
World War II in Europe, *56*

Yom Kippur, 48